# 50

# 50
## Monologues for
## Student Actors

100 monologues
for guys and girls

## MARY DEPNER

MERIWETHER PUBLISHING LTD.
Colorado Springs, Colorado

Meriwether Publishing Ltd., Publisher
PO Box 7710
Colorado Springs, CO 80933-7710

www.meriwether.com

Editor: Theodore O. Zapel
Assistant editor: Amy Hammelev
Cover design: Jan Melvin

Library of Congress Cataloging-in-Publication Data

Depner, Mary.
50/50 monologues for student actors : 100 monologues for guys and girls / by Mary Depner. -- 1st ed.
p. cm.
ISBN 978-1-56608-176-4
1. Monologues. 2. Acting--Auditions. I. Title. II. Title: Fifty/fifty monologues for student actors.
PN2080.D465 2011
808.82'45--dc22
2010049110

1   2   3        11   12   13

*This book is dedicated to my brother Stefan.*

*Just as I said so many times to*

*my parents when we were kids,*

*"This book is all his fault!"*

# Table of Contents

## Monologues for Guys .....................111

# Monologues
# for Girls

# 1. Toes for Two

1    *(MATILDA is getting a manicure and pedicure for her birthday.*
2    *Sitting next to her is her best friend "Lisette." They chat while*
3    *their toes soak and feet get pummeled to perfection.)*
4
5    **Lisette, do you think this will be a good color for my toes**
6    **too?** *(Showing her fingernails to "Lisette")* **Yeah, that's true.**
7    *(Looks down at the nail tech, who's doing her toes.)* **I don't want**
8    **this color on my toenails. I want my toenails to be black.**
9    *(Glances sideways at "Lisette" and giggles. Explaining to the nail*
10   *tech)* **Black and red are our school colors.** *(Pause as she*
11   *listens)* **Yes, we go to Murray Middle. Uh-huh. Eighth grade.**
12   **I'm thirteen. Well, I mean, tomorrow I'll be thirteen. My mom**
13   **gave me this day at the salon for my birthday. I've never had**
14   **a pedicure before, but Lisette has, right Lisette?** *(She glances*
15   *at "Lisette" and smiles. To the nail tech)* **We're best friends.**
16   *(Looks over suddenly at "Lisette" in disbelief.)* **What?!** *(Looks*
17   *embarrassed.)* **You're joking, right? Since when?** *(To the nail*
18   *tech)* **Well, I thought we were best friends.** *(Looks over at*
19   *"Lisette.")* **So, who is she? Huh? Who is your new best friend?**
20   *(Pause)*
21   **Abbey Finegold?** *(Getting loud)* **Abbey Finegold?!** *(Sees*
22   *other patrons looking over and quiets down to a whisper.)* **Abbey**
23   **Finegold has never even been your friend at all and suddenly**
24   **she's your BFF? In fact, last year you listed her as your**
25   **number one frenemy. In your diary, remember?** *(Looks down*
26   *at the nail tech and sighs impatiently.)* **A frenemy is someone**
27   **who pretends to be your friend, but she's really your enemy.**
28   **You know, always talking behind your back and secretly**

1 trying to get you in trouble. That sort of thing. Or you know,
2 someone who doesn't really like you at all, but pretends to
3 just so they can use you. *(Having an epiphany)* **A frenemy is**
4 **someone who purposely shows you an excerpt from her**
5 **diary that lists you as her best friend, just so you'll invite**
6 **her to your day at the spa for her thirteenth birthday!**
7 *("Lisette" tries to speak in her own defense, but MATILDA*
8 *gives her the hand.)* **Don't even try to deny it, Lisette.**
9 *("Lisette" tries to explain again, but MATILDA tries to drown her*
10 *out, putting her fingers in her ears and singing.)* **Lalalala, I'm not**
11 **hearing you.** *(Suddenly looks down at the nail tech.)* **Huh?**
12 *(Quickly pulls her fingers out of her ears and looks at her nails.)*
13 **Oh, shoot!** *(To "Lisette")* **Now look what you made me do!** *(To*
14 *the nail tech in desperation)* **Can you do these two over?**
15 **Please? My mother will kill me. Oh, thank you. No, I promise**
16 **I'll be careful this time. My toes are done?** *(Pulls one foot up*
17 *close to her.)* **Beautiful!** *(Begrudgingly looks over at "Lisette.")*
18 **You were right about the black. It does look really cool.**
19 *(Placing her hand next to her foot)* **Black and red. Awesome!**
20 *(Holds one finger out for the nail tech to fix the smudge.)*
21 Oh, Lisette, there's your mom. OK. See you at the party
22 tomorrow. Yes, you're still invited. *("Lisette" starts to walk*
23 *away.)* **Hey, Lisette, why don't you bring Abbey? Yeah,**
24 **seriously. You know growing up is about a lot more than**
25 **getting a mani/pedi like our moms. OK. Yeah, ask her and**
26 **see if she can. OK. Bye.** *(Holds other finger out for the nail*
27 *tech.)* **Oh, thank you. Yes, it was the mature thing to do. I**
28 **know, most thirteen-year-olds wouldn't even think of it. But**
29 **hey, I'm smarter than most thirteen-year-olds. Lisette's**
30 **mother always makes sure she brings a really nice gift to my**
31 **parties. And as for Abbey, hey, two gifts are better than one.**
32 **I make a pretty good frenemy, don't I? Maybe Lisette and I**
33 **are still BFFs after all. Best Frenemies Forever.**

# 2. The Big Cheese

1  When I started fourth grade I was so excited, because I
2  had been assigned to Mrs. Rickles' class. Mrs. Rickles was
3  well known at our elementary school for being a great
4  teacher who did a lot of fun things with her class. One of the
5  things that I had always heard about from my older brothers
6  and sisters was that Mrs. Rickles assigned a Big Cheese
7  every day of the school year. The Big Cheese got to do
8  special things all day long. Like be the line leader at lunch
9  or pick the game that everybody had to play at recess. So,
10 when I got my turn to be in Mrs. Rickles' class, I was really
11 looking forward to being the Big Cheese. I got to be the Big
12 Cheese the third day of school and it was a lot of fun.

13     By the time our first month of school was over, everyone
14 in the room had been Big Cheese so we were all looking
15 forward to our second turn when October rolled around. It
16 was the first day of October as a matter of fact when we all
17 stood in line outside our classroom door, waiting for the first
18 bell to ring, trying to guess who would be the first to get a
19 second turn at being the Big Cheese. Then the bell rang, the
20 door opened, and we all ran inside to get our seats and to
21 get a look at the Big Cheese's name on the board. But,
22 when we looked at the board, there was a name under the
23 "Big Cheese" title that nobody recognized. It was Ronald
24 Rhinestone. Tommy Johnson's hand shot up in the air.
25 "Mrs. Rickles?" Tommy asked, "Who is Ronald Rhinestone?
26 Do we have a new student in our class?"

27     Mrs. Rickles looked disappointed and shook her head.
28 "Tommy! I'm surprised at you. Ronald's seat has been next

1   to yours since the first day of school. Don't you pay
2   attention to what's going on around you?" She started
3   organizing our reading books for our lesson and we all just
4   stared at each other. The desk next to Tommy was the only
5   one that had been empty since the first day of school. Had
6   Mrs. Rickles flipped her lid?
7      Mrs. Rickles looked at her watch, then she looked at the
8   empty chair. "Ronald, since you are the Big Cheese today,
9   please stand and lead us in the Pledge of Allegiance."
10 Turning, she placed her hand over her heart and began the
11 pledge. But none of us kids moved. We were all speechless.
12 Mrs. Rickles turned and glared and said, "Class! We are
13 saying the pledge! Please stand up!" We all jumped to our
14 feet and started in. When we had finished, Mrs. Rickles said,
15 "That's five minutes shaved off of recess for being ... " She
16 searched for the right words. "Disobedient. Unpatriotic. Just
17 plain rude. And not following the rules. When the Big Cheese
18 stands up for the pledge, everybody stands up for the
19 pledge." Then she looked at the empty chair. "Thank you,
20 Ronald. You can have an extra five minutes of free time in
21 class today to make up for the missed time in recess."
22     We all stared at each other quietly, except for Misty
23 Green who giggled. Mrs. Rickles looked at Misty over the top
24 of her bifocals. Then she said to the empty chair, "Ronald,
25 would you like to pass out the reading books or would you
26 like Misty to do it for you?" She smiled. "Very good." Misty's
27 eyes were as big as saucers. She didn't know what to do.
28 She started to raise her hand, but before she could, Mrs.
29 Rickles said, "Misty, what are you waiting for? The Big
30 Cheese has spoken. Please pass out the books."
31     This was too much for me. I had to do something about
32 this before Mrs. Rickles really went off her rocker. I raised
33 my hand and said, "Mrs. Rickles, may I go to the clinic? I
34 think I'm going to throw up." Mrs. Rickles quickly said,
35 "Yes, of course dear," as she whisked me to the door with a

1 pass in my hand. But just before I got out the door she said,
2 "Ronald, as Big Cheese, would you please escort Lili to the
3 clinic and make sure she gets there OK?" I gulped, but I
4 waited a moment so that "Ronald" could join me and I left
5 the room.

6 Walking to the clinic was weird. I walked faster than I
7 ever have before. When I got there I was out of breath and
8 when I saw Mrs. Battlesides, the principal's secretary, I
9 rushed up to her and blurted out, "Mrs. Rickles has a
10 student in her class today that she calls Ronald
11 Rhinestone." I didn't know what else to say.

12 Mrs. Battlesides looked at me, shrugged, and smiled.
13 "Yes," she said, "I know Ronald very well. He's one of our
14 best students. In fact, this month he's on the Principal's
15 Roll of Honor and Mrs. Rickles has just recommended him
16 for the school patrol squad." She gave me a strange look.
17 "Are you feeling all right dear?"

18 I shook my head. "No. I mean, yes. I mean, I'm fine," I
19 said.

20 "Well, run along back to class then. I'm not really sure
21 what in the world you're doing here," she said.

22 I walked back to class slowly, thinking it all over. When
23 I got to the door I took a deep breath, opened it, and went
24 to my assigned seat next to Amy Linehimer. Amy leaned
25 over and asked, "What happened?" I looked over at her
26 coyly, and grinning, I whispered, "Ronald kissed me."

# 3. The Runaway

1      I ran away from home last year around Christmastime.
2    Well, yeah, it's Christmastime now, so it was about a year
3    ago. Yeah, a year ago I ran away from home. Is that better?
4    More precise? You know, I'm supposed to be able to "speak
5    freely here" without criticism and I barely get a sentence out
6    when you're butting in. You know, I should just keep my
7    mouth shut like freak boy does over there. Sorry, Freddy. I
8    meant to say Freddy and freak boy just slipped out. Oops.
9    Sorry again. Well, anyway, is this my turn to talk or what?
10   Then please, may I ask nicely that you don't interrupt me?
11   Thank you, your royal highness. I mean Madame Counselor
12   or whatever you are. OK, Bridgette. Geez. Do you really
13   want us to call you Bridgette? I mean, you're like a hundred
14   years older than anybody else in this room. Maybe we
15   should call you granny.
16      Oh really? I'm not upsetting you? I'm just trying to get
17   attention? You make me want to pull every single hair out of
18   my head. Of course I'm upsetting you. But I'm supposed to
19   be talking about me! This is my time to think about me and
20   why I ran away. Right? So why are we talking about you and
21   how you're not upset and what you think I'm trying to do?
22   You know, freak boy, you are really on to something with the
23   silent game. Don't say a word for her. She'll just try to
24   annoy you. *(Takes a huge breath.)* Sorry, freak boy. I meant
25   Freddy. *(She laughs at her own humor, then shakes her head.)*
26      OK, you know what, Bridgette. Today is your lucky day
27   'cause I am going to talk. I am going to give you the grand
28   prize of all prizes. I am going to get everything off my chest

1 for the first and the last time in my entire life! And you will
2 be the queen of this place. The one that broke Amanda —
3 the weird girl, the crazy girl, the runaway. Yeah, why not.
4 You look like someone who never had much luck. Why else
5 would you be in this hole with seven pimply adolescents who
6 the rest of the world can't stand. OK, so for you, unlucky
7 Bridgette, today the wind is gonna change.

8     You know *(Laughing)* like in that old movie when the
9 wind changed and the kids got lucky and got the really cool
10 nanny that made them float. Hey, maybe she gave them
11 drugs or something. Do ya think? Maybe the cool nanny was
12 really a pusher and nobody gets it but me. *(Laughing until*
13 *she becomes very silent)* OK, the big secret. I ran away from
14 home because everybody in my family is screwed up and I
15 felt scared and alone and I had no choice. Now, what are you
16 going to do about it? Give me a big group hug and send me
17 back home? Or put me in a foster home where chances are
18 it will be no better, probably worse? Why am I here like I'm
19 the broken one? Huh, Freaky Freddy, do you know? Say
20 something! Is it my fault that the world I was born into is
21 rotten like last year's garbage? Do you think I chose to be a
22 runaway?

# 4. Rainy Days

1     When it rains I like to play a game. It's this game where
2  I take these five characters, these five girls I made up in my
3  head, and I imagine what they are doing. Unlike me, who is
4  sitting on the couch, looking out the window with nothing to
5  do, no one to talk to but the cat, my characters lead exciting
6  lives on rainy days.

7     For instance, Emma. Emma is a beautiful brunette with
8  long silky hair and dark eyes. When it rains, Emma's
9  boyfriend Rodrigo comes over in his little red Corvette and
10  takes her for a drive. They love the rain because it reminds
11  them of the first day they met. She went out for a walk in
12  the beautiful English countryside where she lives and
13  suddenly a storm came up out of the blue. Within moments
14  she was drenched. Having gone quite far from home, she
15  didn't know what to do. Seek shelter under a tree and wait
16  out the storm or try to head back toward her family's lovely
17  English manor? Suddenly, Rodrigo pulled up on a big black
18  horse. It reminded her of something from a storybook. Like
19  he was a knight in shining armor. He jumped off his horse,
20  took off his cloak and covered her, then asked if he could
21  give her a ride. Of course she said yes. They galloped home
22  through the rain and the rest is history.

23     Then there's Amelia. Amelia loves the rain because she
24  used to be a mermaid. Used to be because she fell in love
25  with a human and made a wish to be able to marry him and
26  live on land. But, even though Amelia is happy with her new
27  life, she loves the rain because she can go out in it and feel
28  like she used to feel as she swam through the ocean and
29  played with the fish.

1   Yes, so that's Amelia, out walking somewhere right now,
2   playing in puddles and getting drenched and loving every
3   second. She'll probably run into Delila, as a matter of fact.
4   Delila loves the rain because she is always looking for frogs
5   to kiss so that she can find her prince. You see, Delila had
6   her fortune told when she was very young and she knows
7   without a shadow of a doubt that one day she will marry a
8   prince and live happily ever after. So, she is always on the
9   lookout for that prince who she is most certainly sure has
10  disguised himself as a frog. And what better way to find
11  frogs than out in the rain?
12      Now Kansas is a different story. She's a farmer whose
13  crops are always thirsty and can't ever seem to get enough
14  to drink. When it rains she is so filled with joy that she goes
15  out and dances in the storm as she sings her praises to the
16  sky.
17      And then there's number five. The fifth girl is Cody. The
18  kindest soul that ever lived. When it rains, Cody gets busy
19  and collects every single drop that she can so that she can
20  bring it to people in parts of the world that have no water.
21      Hmmmm. Don't you love a rainy day?

# 5. Tennis, Anyone?

1      I love tennis. And, as my mother would say, that is the
2  understatement of the year. I live, eat, breathe, and sleep
3  the game. How do I sleep the game? It's in my dreams,
4  da'ling! *(Laughs.)* It's in my dreams and it's the first thing
5  on my mind when I wake up. What do I dream? Oh gosh! It
6  varies, but usually I'm playing somebody great, like Venus
7  or Serena. And, yes, I'm usually winning. Of course.

8      I think tennis is a lot like life. Well, I mean, at least I
9  think it's a lot like life in some ways and in other ways it's
10  a lot like life should be. Well, OK, the part that's like life is
11  the sweet spot. You know, there's a place on the racquet
12  that's the sweet spot. When the ball meets the sweet spot
13  you're in control. I see life like that, 'cause I see people like
14  the ball. Everybody lands somewhere and some of us land
15  in the sweet spot and some of us don't. When you're in the
16  sweet spot you make friends easily and things go your way.
17  When you aren't in the sweet spot, it's like you're swimming
18  up stream. You can try to make it work, but the only way to
19  find your sweet spot is to keep looking for another place to
20  be.

21      You have this look on your face that says I'm speaking
22  Greek. Well, maybe I can better explain how life should be
23  like tennis.

24      In tennis, opponents stay on their side of the net. They
25  can argue, they can fight the fight, without ever crossing
26  into their opponent's territory. That's how life should be.
27  And when it's all over, they are both still standing and they
28  even shake hands. Now that's dignified. And the best part

1 of tennis, when a player doesn't have anything, they still
2 have Love. In fact, everybody starts with Love. Isn't that
3 how life should be? I mean, I went to the hospital last week
4 to see my new niece. Yeah, my brother Louie and his wife
5 had the cutest baby girl. But ya know, I looked in at the
6 nursery and saw little Ellie and I looked at all the babies and
7 I thought, "Wow, I hope they all start out with love." In
8 tennis you can be sure, but in life? You just never know.

# 6. The Betrayal

1     Did you ever get writer's block? It's when you sit down
2 to write something and nothing comes out. I mean, you
3 might be the greatest writer in this world, but suddenly you
4 draw a blank. You look at the paper after an hour, or your
5 computer screen, and zilch, nada, nothing.
6     No, I don't think it happens when you text somebody. I
7 don't know, maybe. It doesn't happen to me when I text, but
8 it happened to me last week in Mr. Robinson's English
9 class. Mr. Robinson is the best teacher I've ever had. He
10 thinks I have talent. As a writer, I mean. He's always telling
11 me that. So, anyway, he does this thing every now and then
12 where he stops the lesson and gives us a surprise writing
13 assignment. It's kind of like a pop quiz, but it's a writing
14 assignment. He says, "Pull out some paper and a pencil.
15 Here's a topic — now go." Then he stops you after ten
16 minutes and asks you to turn it in.
17     Well, last week he writes on the board, "Tell me about
18 the worst betrayal you've ever witnessed, heard about, or
19 experienced." Now that's a pretty serious topic, right? Well,
20 the weird thing is, just the night before, my friend Kirsten
21 had confided in me about her brother. He stole the family's
22 vacation fund and used it to buy stuff for his car. He let
23 them think that the house was broken into and he almost
24 got away with it. Well, he sort of did get away with it. Only
25 Kirsten knows. She doesn't know what to do. Well, anyway,
26 she made me swear up and down that I wouldn't tell
27 anybody. So I did. I mean, I swore. But then, when Mr.
28 Robinson put that topic on the board, I drew a blank. Except

1   for Kristen's story. It's like it kept drowning everything out
2   and wouldn't let anything else in my head. The clock was
3   ticking away and I got desperate. I guess I shouldn't have
4   used Kristen's name, though. Now Mr. Robinson knows and
5   called me aside the next day. He said he's got to talk to
6   Kristen about it. And to her parents, too. He says it's the
7   right thing to do. *(Pause)* I broke my promise and now I've
8   got to brace myself. I'm sure I've lost a friend. And it only
9   took me less than ten minutes.

# 7. Who's Not That into Who?

1     Hey, Mom, are you crying? What's wrong? What
2  happened? *(Listens.)* Oh. How long has it been since he
3  called? Two days? Well, hey, that's not that long. It is? You
4  are? Don't say that. Don't give up. There'll be lots of other
5  guys. Besides, he's probably going to call tonight. He's
6  probably got a lot of stuff to do and — what? He's just not
7  that into you? Oh, geez! I hate that saying. I mean, maybe
8  you're not that into him. Or maybe you shouldn't be. Maybe
9  he's a jerk. Maybe you've really got a million other things to
10 do than wait for him to give you a call. You texted him?
11 Yesterday? Really? And he didn't answer? Hmmmm. Well,
12 maybe his phone got lost. Or maybe he did what I did last
13 year and he dropped it in the tub and it's fried. Yeah,
14 remember? See, there's a million and one reasons he may
15 not have gotten your text. Or he got it, but hasn't been able
16 to text you back for some crazy reason.

17     So, why are you still crying? You are pretty! You are! And
18 you're fun to be around. Uh-huh. Yes, you definitely are.
19 Everybody thinks so. You're smart too. And funny! Yeah,
20 remember yesterday when you made everybody laugh. That
21 macaroni and cheese joke. Remember? That was so funny.
22 And you're talented too. You have the prettiest voice. And
23 the prettiest hair. Of course he's into you. If he's not into
24 you, he's crazy.

25    *(Pausing to think)* You know, maybe the problem isn't you
26 at all. Maybe the problem is me. Mom, it's true. I'm a pain
27 in the neck sometimes. Especially lately. Maybe if I weren't
28 in the picture you'd be out with him tonight. Maybe he's not

1  that into me. Did you ever think about that? *(Listens.)* You're
2  right, he is a jerk if he doesn't like me. *(Laughs softly.)* I
3  know, I know, I wouldn't let anyone come between us either.
4  Well, maybe he's just never had kids and doesn't
5  understand that we have this bond. Maybe he's jealous.
6  *(Smiles.)* You're right, maybe we should go to a movie. Hey,
7  is that your cell phone? It's him? Aren't you going to answer
8  it? Oh. Good idea. Yeah, call him tomorrow. Or next week.
9  *(Laughs. Walking off together)* Hey, what movie do you want
10 to see?

# 8. Curiosity and Cashews

1   Did you ever wonder where cashews come from?
2   Cashews. You know, the nut. No, not that guy in first period.
3   The other nut. The one that comes in a can. Did you ever
4   wonder where it originally came from? Like, before it got in
5   the can? Dude, if you'd take those things out of your ears
6   and listen for a minute, you'd be able to understand the
7   question. Thank you. The question is, do you know where
8   cashews come from? No, before the grocery store. Before
9   the store! OK, so the answer is "no." You do not know. Yes,
10  I know. I know because one night, I was sitting in bed eating
11  cashews and I suddenly had this curious thought. I mean,
12  here I am spending my whole life in this state of un-
13  curiosity, when — *(Gets interrupted)* I know that's not a word,
14  but I just made it up, so now it is a word. Un-curiosity is the
15  state of being totally uncurious about anything and
16  everything in the world around you. Oh, shut up. I don't care
17  if uncurious is a word. You're making me lose my train of
18  thought. Where was I? Oh yeah, in bed. I was eating these
19  cashews in bed one night and I suddenly realized that I had
20  no idea how they grew. And suddenly, I had to know. Yes, I
21  had to. Or I would have exploded! Let me finish the story.

22      So, I searched for them on the web and found out. It was
23  incredible. It was the weirdest thing. I mean, I would never
24  have guessed that's how they grew. I bet you a million
25  dollars you could ask one hundred people on the street and
26  they wouldn't know. You could do one of those late night TV
27  things where they go out and talk to total strangers, and I
28  guarantee that no one would have a clue. Why? Because

1   most people are like me. Well, like the old me, before the
2   cashew awakening. *(Thinks for a moment.)* Their un-curiosity
3   is their defining trait. They just don't care. I mean, they just
4   take everything for granted. Cashews are just the tip of the
5   iceberg, ya know? Hmmmm? Am I going to tell you? Tell you
6   what? Where they come from? Icebergs? Ohhhh. Cashews.
7   No. Yes, I said no. Why? Because every man, or woman,
8   must de-ignorify themselves. De-ignorify! Of course it's not
9   a word, but I just made it up, so now it is one.

# 9. Would You Read the Label?

1     Wouldn't it be great if people were like food? I mean
2   *(Laughs)* no, not like for cannibals. I mean, wouldn't it be
3   cool if people had labels on them like food? You know, you
4   go to the grocery store and you read the labels to see if it's
5   all natural or if the stuff is full of a bunch of junk. Artificial
6   colors, trans fat. It's like, last summer I met this guy at the
7   beach and he looked so hot. If he were food, I would have
8   thought he'd be like all natural with definitely no fat. But
9   after a few weeks I found out that he was the opposite. He
10  was, like, artificial everything and full of sugar, too. You
11  know, sugar gives you that energy spike, but then eventually
12  drops you down real low. And the things he'd spent his free
13  time doing didn't impress me too much. I mean, the more I
14  found out about him the less thrilled I was that we met. That
15  would be the best thing to see on a label. A guy's life story.
16  No secrets. Nothing held back. So, you'd be like, OK this
17  guy looks really cool, but he's an idiot.
18     I don't know, maybe it wouldn't be that much help at all.
19  I mean sometimes something just looks so delicious I don't
20  even care what the label says. Like a big frozen pizza, or
21  some gooey chocolate cake. In fact, sometimes I just don't
22  want to know. And, if some hot guy is staring me in the
23  face, asking me to go out Friday night, even if I have a
24  hunch that the relationship is not going to be good for me,
25  do I really care at that moment? Think about it. If you had
26  the chance to date the cutest guy in school, would you read
27  the label?

# 10. Better Left Unsaid

1     My mom and I had lunch yesterday. Yeah, I know, it
2 sounds like no big deal. But my story is a little different and
3 it was a really, really big deal. You see, my mom left when I
4 was a kid, and yesterday was the first time that I'd seen her
5 in ten years.
6     Uh-huh. Ten years. Yeah, it was pretty emotional. I guess
7 more for her than for me. Although, everyone says that I
8 suppress my emotions. That I deny my feelings. But hey, it's
9 been ten years and I've had ten years to work on
10 suppressing my emotions. So I did a pretty good job of it
11 yesterday. Was I excited? Well, a little. Mostly because I
12 wanted some answers and I was really looking forward to
13 asking her questions that I've been asking myself ever since
14 she left. Like what happened? Why did you leave? Why
15 didn't you even say good-bye?
16     It was always a mystery to me. My dad never wanted to
17 talk about it and I'm not sure he really knew the story
18 anyway. That is, her side of the story.
19     For me, I always liked to try to imagine what had
20 happened. I knew that my mother wouldn't leave unless
21 something really huge had happened. Something beyond her
22 control, like maybe she witnessed a crime and had to be
23 placed in protective custody. Or she was being threatened
24 by the mob and had to leave to protect us. Yeah, I watch a
25 lot of TV. But the other thing I used to imagine was some
26 romantic story. Like, some gorgeous guy from her past had
27 shown up and swept her away. She loved us, but couldn't
28 stay because it would hurt my dad too much to see her with

1   this new guy, so she'd just disappeared. I would sometimes
2   daydream that she was living in some wonderful place with
3   this man. Like Paris or somewhere in Italy. She was very
4   happy, but every day she would cry at least once and she'd
5   dream of the day when she could come back and be with us
6   all. And I knew in my heart that my dad would forgive her
7   and we'd all be a family again.
8       So, what happened? Why did she leave? Why did she
9   come back? Well, those are the first things I asked her of
10  course, but I didn't get the answers that I'd expected.
11      She said that the day she left she'd been at work and
12  had gone to lunch at a little café. She said that everything
13  in her life seemed like it had no purpose. She wondered what
14  would happen if she just didn't go back to work that day.
15  Then she realized that she'd have to go home and tell my
16  dad that she'd left her job. She'd have to spend her days
17  just cleaning and taking care of us kids and she felt like
18  somewhere inside she was still a kid herself. That's when
19  she started wondering what would happen if she just never
20  went home. She said she was right near the highway and
21  she had some friends in North Carolina that she knew would
22  let her stay with them for a while. So, she got up from her
23  lunch and she never looked back. She said she didn't want
24  to say good-bye because she couldn't explain her feelings to
25  us. She said that some things are better left unsaid.
26      Well, anyway, she said she had often thought of us kids
27  and wondered how we were, but she always knew deep
28  inside that we were better off.
29      So, I said, "Why did you come here today to see me?"
30  She said she'd gotten a chance to come out to California on
31  a business trip with her boyfriend and she just thought that
32  maybe it was time. Then she actually had the nerve to say,
33  "I'm glad to see you're doing so well." I thought, "How do
34  you know how I'm doing?" We hadn't even said two words
35  about me yet. I said, "If you'll excuse me, I need to use the

1   ladies room." I went to the back of the restaurant where the
2   bathroom was, but that's not where I went. I opened the exit
3   door and headed out. You know, she's right. Some things
4   are better left unsaid.

# 11. They Do

1 Bye Mom! Bye Dad!
2 Wow, that went really well. What? They do like you. They
3 do. Donny, my parents *do like you.* Of course they do. Oh,
4 please. How can you tell they don't like you? They just met
5 you. You guys weren't even in the same room for fifteen
6 minutes, so what in the world could possibly give you that
7 impression?
8 My mom? Oh, that. Of course she didn't smile. She's
9 very focused on anti-aging. She's extremely worried about
10 the wrinkles that she has around her lips. They're smile
11 wrinkles, so she's trying not to smile. When you made that
12 joke she totally wanted to laugh. Of course she did. That
13 was so funny. You couldn't tell, but I could see it. Her
14 stomach. You know it was moving up and down like a
15 chuckle. She totally thought that was funny. "Wet socks on
16 the counter." *(Laughs.)* That was hilarious.
17 Huh? My dad? Oh, he loved you! He didn't say anything?
18 Well, yeah, that's true. But you know why? My dad is the
19 type of person who really likes to choose his words very
20 carefully. He's probably busy right now putting together
21 what he's going to say to you the next time he sees you. Of
22 course he is. No, he is not going to say "Stay away from my
23 daughter." He's probably thinking of something he can
24 invite you to do, like go fishing or something. You know,
25 some guy bonding thing. I'm sure that's what he's busy
26 planning.
27 The dog? Well, that was sort of weird. I mean, honestly,
28 she has never bitten anyone before, but I don't think you

1 should take it personally. How silly would that be? It's kind
2 of like a compliment in a way because she chose to take a
3 bite out of you. You really got her attention, ya know. Some
4 people come in the house and she doesn't even bark. Now
5 *that* I would find highly insulting. My brother, oh, well, he
6 never likes anybody, so he doesn't count in this discussion.
7 Oh, Donny, I am so excited. I was so worried about this
8 meeting and it went so totally well. They like you. They do.
9 They really, really do!

# 12. What Can I Say?

1   *(THERESA is sitting next to a grave at the cemetery with a*
2   *bunch of flowers in her hand. She places a flower on the*
3   *grave, then one on her lap.)*
4

5   **One for you. One for me. Two for you. Two for me.** *(To the*
6   *audience)* **What do you say to someone after they die? I say**
7   **anything that I want. Anything that I wanted to say in life,**
8   **but couldn't. Some things I never thought to say, but should**
9   **have. The question is, do they hear you? Do they know?**
10  *(She gets up and goes to another grave. Kneeling she places*
11  *a flower on the grave.)* **One for you too, Granny Ethel. I love**
12  **you.** *(Chuckles.)* **Remember when I stayed home from school**
13  **with the chicken pox. You took such good care of me. Two**
14  **more for you. I love you Granny.**
15  *(Moves on to another grave.)* **This is Mr. Fischer. He's the**
16  **grocer. Well, he was the grocer. It's strange, but I never**
17  **really thanked him for being so nice to me when I had to**
18  **work after school one year. He always asked me if I had a**
19  **lot of homework and made sure I never had to work too late.**
20  **He said it was a shame when young people had to work and**
21  **couldn't focus on their studies. He said he wished he'd been**
22  **able to study more and maybe even go to college. I hate to**
23  **admit it, but I never really listened when he talked. And he**
24  **had good advice, but I just tuned out most of it. He was**
25  **just another old person who hadn't fulfilled his dreams. But**
26  **he was more than that. He was someone who didn't need to**
27  **care about me, but he did anyway. He could have made me**
28  **work late. He could've not even bothered to know my name.**

1  Here's one for you Mr. Fischer.

2  *(To the audience)* **You know, if there's someone you want**
3  **to say something to, say it. If there's someone who wants**
4  **to say something to you, you might want to listen. Because**
5  **you never know. One day it might be too late. And then you**
6  **can give them a whole lot of your time, a whole lot of your**
7  **love.** *(Sets all of the flowers on a grave.)* **You can even give**
8  **them a whole bouquet. But will they ever know?**

# 13. Love at First Sight

1    *(NATASHA is sitting in English class, raising her hand.)*

2

3    Excuse me Mrs. L, but I just wanted to ask you a
4    question about *Romeo and Juliet*. Yes, I read it. I read it four
5    times as a matter of fact. I am curious about something,
6    Mrs. L. Do you believe in love at first sight? Can two people
7    look across a room at a party and know? I mean, just know.
8    And if that can happen, can it happen anywhere? Like,
9    what if Romeo and Juliet had been at the grocery store? Or
10    in the mall? Do you really think so, Mrs. L? Wow, that is so
11    romantic. That is so cool. The thing is, though, do you really
12    believe it? I mean, in real life, can that really happen? It can?
13    It does? Did it happen to you? Is that how you met Mr. L?
14    Not quite. Hmmmm. Well, no offense, or anything, but if
15    that's not how it happened, what if Mr. L isn't the right
16    person for you? What if one day the two of you are at the
17    movies or in a hardware store and you look up at the guy at
18    the counter and you just know? And he just knows. Then
19    what? I know, I know, that is an inappropriate question. I'm
20    sorry. I just wondered. Gosh. I'm sorry.

21    *(Starts to look through her notebook, but then thinks of*
22    *something else. Raises her hand. "Mrs. L" doesn't notice her, so*
23    *she clears her throat to get her attention.)* **Mrs. L.** Excuse me,
24    Mrs. L. I have one more question. No, this one is not about
25    you and your husband. I promise. I don't know what came
26    over me. I mean, I know you and Mr. L are probably, like,
27    inseparable and all that. No, it's just, this love at first sight
28    thing has really got me. I mean, here we are studying this

1 great play that everyone loves. And if you really love this
2 story, you kind of have to buy into the love at first sight
3 thing. And if you buy into this love at first sight thing, well,
4 it must be that deep down inside everyone kind of thinks it
5 could happen to them. And ... if it can happen, why don't
6 we try to help make it happen? How? Well, by seeing a lot of
7 people. No, not dating. Seeing. We should make it a point to
8 get eye contact with as many people as we possibly can.

9 *(Looks around to the class.)* **Here** we are on the brink of
10 becoming adults. Almost ready to go out in the world to
11 plan our lives. What could be more important than finding
12 your soul mate, your one and only? The *one.* Or, on the
13 other hand, if we have other things we need to do in life first.
14 Like graduate college, for instance. Maybe we should avoid
15 eye contact completely. Until the time is right. Hey, did
16 someone just throw a wad of paper at me? Mrs. L! Are you
17 going to do anything? Who did that?

# 14. Sixteen Candles

1    Last year, a few months before my sixteenth birthday,
2  my dad brought home this old car. It was a little beat up
3  convertible. Dad and my brother had negotiated with
4  someone to get it in exchange for some work. They do that
5  all the time. Get old cars and fix them up. As a hobby, but
6  also for a little extra money.

7    Well, last year, I was turning sixteen and all that, so I
8  was a little suspicious when they started fixing this one up.
9  Usually they just get it running, give it a fresh coat of paint,
10  reupholster the seats with some black plastic vinyl stuff,
11  and put it in the classified ads. They always manage to
12  make enough to take a little fishing trip on the weekend in
13  the Keys.

14    Well, last year, like I said, I was a little suspicious. Here
15  I am, on the verge of turning sixteen, getting my driver's
16  license and all that. Every night they'd work on that car and
17  every morning I'd go out to see what they'd done. This
18  wasn't getting fixed up like their ordinary cars. This was
19  being made ... well, adorable. OK, maybe adorable isn't a
20  good word to describe a car, but it was ... well, it was cool.
21  They gave it a cherry red paint job that shined beyond
22  compare. They put a new canvas top on that was snow
23  white and my dad upholstered the seats in the most
24  beautiful taffy white leather. Oh my gosh. This car was my
25  dream come true. I could just see myself driving up to
26  school on the day after my birthday. No more taking the bus
27  for me.

28    I was so excited that I couldn't sleep the night before. I
29  kept tossing and turning and grinning to myself. It was all I

1 could do to not go out in the garage and look. I didn't want
2 to spoil the surprise in case they'd put a red ribbon on it or
3 anything. Well, the morning of my birthday I woke up and
4 everyone acted like it was just a normal birthday. They all
5 said happy birthday. My mom gave me one small present
6 before I went to school. "Great job of acting," I thought, "I
7 wonder if they are as excited as me?"
8     It was so hard concentrating that day. I don't think I got
9 anything done. And I don't think I cared. Allison, my best
10 friend, asked me for the fifth time what time the birthday
11 party was at my house that night. I wondered out loud,
12 "Hey, are you in on it too?" She just looked at me like I was
13 nuts. "Yep," I thought, "Allison knows." So that night,
14 around seven thirty, all the relatives came over for spaghetti,
15 'cause that's my favorite. Allison and her boyfriend Edward
16 showed up a little bit late. They just can't be on time.
17 Finally, after eating and blowing out the candles on my
18 cake, the big moment arrived. The gifts. One after another,
19 I opened them all. Wow, they were really building up the
20 suspense.
21     When I had opened the last one, Grandma Reilly said,
22 "Well, pumpkin, Grandpa and I'd better get going. This sure
23 was fun, but it is way past our bedtime."
24     "Going?" I said. "You can't. I mean, not yet. Right Mom?
25 Right Dad?"
26     "Grandma needs her sleep too, you know. Is my little girl
27 not wanting to grow up?"
28     "No, no," I said. "I just don't want you to miss
29 anything."
30     Mom was cleaning up the wrapping paper and Aunt Tess
31 started doing the dishes. Aunt Tess looked back at me and
32 said, "You're lucky you're the birthday girl, honey, this sink
33 is a mess." Well, as hard as it was to believe, Grandma and
34 Grandpa Reilly left. Aunt Tess finished the dishes and fell
35 asleep on the couch. Allison and Edward asked me if I

1    wanted to go for a ride to the beach. OK, this is it, I thought.
2    "A ride?" I said. "OK. Who's driving?"
3         They looked at me like I was nuts. "Edward," Allison
4    said.
5         "Oh yeah," I muttered. I went for a ride to the beach in
6    Edward's pickup truck. Allison sat smushed in the middle.
7    The next morning I woke up and caught the bus. My dad and
8    my brother sold the little red convertible the next week and
9    no one had a clue that it should have been mine.

# 15. A Central Park Moon

1    I'll always remember the Central Park moon. The night I
2 saw that moon was the first night that I felt really happy
3 again. It was the first sign that my life could be happy after
4 all the stuff that had taken place.

5    Until I was nine, things in my life were great. My family
6 ... it's hard to talk about it even now, but my family was
7 perfect. There really isn't any other word for it.

8    We were like a little team, Mom, Dad, me, and Peter.
9 Just the four of us. Dad was a college professor for Littleton
10 Community College. He taught theatre and every summer he
11 directed the Children's Theatre Summer Camp. Peter and I
12 always attended and by the time I was nine I'd had the lead
13 role in three plays. I always felt like Dad's little princess. His
14 little leading lady.

15    My mom's a musician. She plays just about every
16 instrument you can think of, but piano is really her thing.
17 She always wanted to be home for us kids, so she taught
18 piano in her studio on the second floor of our house. Things
19 in our house were like her little metronome — it all just
20 went along like clockwork. Until my ninth birthday.

21    It was supposed to be a great day. We had invited
22 Grandma and Grandpa over and there was this huge box
23 wrapped in pink sitting in the middle of the living room floor.
24 Peter had helped Mom make the cake and he was really
25 excited. It was pink, too, and about seven layers high. It was
26 a little lopsided, but pretty cool. I had just blown out the
27 candles on the cake when there was a knock at the door. I
28 didn't pay attention at first when Mom went to answer it.

1   But when she came back she looked kind of white like she'd
2   just seen a ghost. She told my dad that one of his students
3   needed to see him. I watched Dad go to the door and I could
4   see who it was through the screen. I had seen her before a
5   million times. She was in this Shakespeare play my dad had
6   directed in the fall. Peter and I had gone with Dad a bunch
7   of times to watch rehearsals. Now, I could see her face and
8   it looked like she'd been crying.

9       After about five minutes Dad came in and she was gone,
10  but everything had changed. Grandma and Grandpa tried to
11  act like nothing was wrong, but Mom and Dad didn't say
12  another word. Not to each other. Not to anybody. I opened
13  the big pink box on the floor and it was exactly what I
14  wanted. But suddenly I didn't care anymore. I had this
15  feeling in the pit of my stomach that my whole world had
16  just exploded and was falling back down to the earth in a
17  million pieces. And I was right. After that day, my life would
18  never be the same. Late that night, I heard my parents
19  fighting and my mom crying harder than I'd ever heard her
20  cry before. I came out of my room for a minute and my dad
21  passed me in the hall with a suitcase. He had tears in his
22  eyes and he tried to speak, but it seemed too hard. He
23  brushed past me and walked out the front door.

24      Nothing in my life was the same after that day. After
25  that, I hated my birthday. Every year I insisted that we not
26  have a cake. Mom didn't argue. It wasn't her favorite day
27  either, I suppose.

28      But last year, for my sixteenth birthday, my Aunt Anne
29  invited me to New York City to see a play and spend the
30  weekend with her. We saw a wonderful show and afterwards
31  went to a party. It was in an apartment that my aunt
32  described as "charming." I'd never really heard anyone use
33  that word before, but you know what, she was right. It was
34  charming.

35      During the party, I walked out on the balcony and I

1   looked out over Central Park. It looked magical and it was
2   being lit by the most beautiful moon I had ever seen. The
3   biggest moon I'd ever seen. I stared at that moon and it was
4   like ... it was like it was talking to me. That night the moon
5   told me that I would be happy again. From that moment on.
6   Just me. In my life. A separate life. All my own. That night,
7   that moon made a promise to me. A promise that my life
8   could be ... would be ... charming. And for the first time in
9   a long time, I felt peaceful, serene, and secure. I never
10 thought I'd feel that way again. It had taken seven years, but
11 it was definitely worth the wait.

# 16. The Idiot's Daughter

1    We used to have this neighbor who hated my dad. It was
2    all because of one stupid thing. He complained to the county
3    about her rooster crowing at four o'clock in the morning and
4    the county officials came and took it away. Only thing is,
5    they also took her chickens. I mean, it's not like we live on
6    a farm. It's just that we have big yards in my neighborhood
7    and people can pretty much do what they want. We like it
8    that way, and the thing is we used to have chickens too, but
9    not a rooster. A rooster is a completely different story!
10   Anyway, one day I came home from school and my
11   neighbor came storming out of our house. She looked at me
12   and said, "Your father is an idiot." I was a little bit shocked,
13   but I had the sense to shout after her, "That idiot's done a
14   lot for you." And he had. I mean, with the exception of
15   getting her chickens confiscated, he loaned her ladders,
16   helped her fix her leaking ceiling, had her kids over for meals
17   about a hundred times. That's 'cause they were always
18   hanging around at dinnertime, when she was too busy
19   working on junk in her yard or something.
20   Oh yeah, I forgot to mention *that*, didn't I? She used to
21   collect junk that she would turn into "yard art" or
22   "sculptures," as she liked to call them. My mother called
23   them gar-bazh. That's sort of French for garbage. So, our
24   lovely neighbor made a lot of trips to the junkyard and since
25   her husband went "missing" at some point, it seemed like
26   she liked to pick up friends at the junkyard too. Other artsy
27   types that were pretty strange. So, I think her kids didn't
28   like to be at home as much as they liked to be at our house.

1   I couldn't blame them.

2   Anyway, that one day she looked at me and called my
3   dad an idiot, she never apologized, or said she regretted it,
4   or anything. I didn't say anything to anybody, but it kind of
5   festered in me. This completely wrong act. Here was an
6   adult acting worse than a twelve-year-old. Saying something
7   that I would never say to another kid even if it might have
8   been true.

9   Well, anyway, one day she and her kids moved away. The
10  junk was removed from the yard and some other family
11  moved in that I can't remember. I sort of missed the kids
12  when they were gone. And I never saw them again.

13  But one day I was at the mall and I saw *her*. She was all
14  alone and looked about a hundred years older. I tried to get
15  past without her noticing me, but our eyes met and her face
16  immediately lit up. She walked up to me like she was
17  remembering an old friend. She's like, "Elizabeth, how are
18  you?" I stood there for a moment just thinking. Then I said,
19  "You must be mistaken, ma'am, I'm not Elizabeth, I'm the
20  idiot's daughter." Then I walked past her without another
21  word. There are some things you just can't forgive and
22  forget.

# 17. Conversation from a First Date

1     I've had some weird first dates. Probably the reason that
2 I haven't had too many second dates, but hey, that's beside
3 the point. My first dates have at least been really
4 memorable. For example, there was the guy that my cousin
5 Lisa set me up with when I spent the summer with her in
6 Dallas last year. He was a little too old for me, but that just
7 made him more intriguing. So, we met at this really fancy
8 steakhouse for lunch on Sunday afternoon. He was dressed
9 in a very cool shirt and jeans. I wore this red skirt and a
10 black T-shirt. I thought we looked really awesome together,
11 but I wasn't sure what he thought. He kind of looked down
12 a lot and mumbled. Then half way through our meal he said,
13 "If you were a piece of fruit, what would you be?"
14     I said, "Excuse me?" I wasn't sure that I heard him right.
15 He said it again and I laughed. I thought, "This guy's pretty
16 funny," but then I looked at him and he wasn't even
17 cracking a smile. He was dead serious. So ... I said, "Well,
18 Jason," that was his name, "I never really thought about it
19 before, but I think I would be an apple."
20     "An apple?" he said, looking somewhat disappointed, I
21 believe. "Why?"
22     "Well, I guess, I like apples?" I was searching for a
23 reason, but to tell you the truth I had kind of picked the
24 apple randomly.
25     Suddenly, he blurted out, "I'm a banana!" Then he
26 looked embarrassed and looked down at his plate. "I mean,
27 I'd be a banana. If I were a fruit."
28     "Ummmm. Oh," I said. "Why a banana, Jason?" I have
29 to admit, he had piqued my curiosity.

1 He cleared his throat and looked around to make sure
2 that no one could hear him. "I'm not what I seem to be," he
3 said. "I'm waiting to find the right person or the right
4 circumstance in life ... that will ... peel me, so to speak, and
5 reveal my true self." His eyes were staring into mine with a
6 look of complete and utter sincerity. I wanted to do one of
7 three things: get up and run, explode with laughter, or say
8 "You are the strangest person I've ever met!" But instead I
9 just looked at my watch and said, "I don't think I can have
10 dessert, Jason. I've got something to do later on and I need
11 to get going soon." He seemed disappointed that I wasn't
12 going to take the banana conversation any further. He asked
13 if he could call me again and I said, "I'm going back home
14 to Savannah soon, but maybe we'll bump into each other
15 next summer." I was never so relieved to be out of a
16 restaurant and on my way home. Later that night, though, I
17 couldn't get our conversation out of my head. I just kept
18 thinking, "If I were a fruit, what kind would I be?"

# 18. Missing

1     You know how in your American history book you read
2    about the shot heard around the world? You don't? Were you
3    awake in American history? Well, anyway, maybe it struck
4    me more because I could relate. I don't know how to fire a
5    gun and I don't want to know. Unfortunately, it isn't only a
6    gunshot that can be heard around the world. It could be
7    something you say. Something you do.

8     I did something one day that changed my world, the
9    world of my family, and most of all the world of my best
10   friend's family. My best friend who I haven't seen since that
11   day.

12    It was her birthday and like the year before and the year
13   before that we were at Tyler Park with Amy's mom. Her
14   mom had a really hard job and she liked to let Amy invite a
15   few friends to the park for her birthday. Then, she'd lie on a
16   hammock and read while we went off for adventures,
17   climbing rocks, renting canoes, or swimming in the lake.
18   One thing we always loved to do was walk the nature path
19   that took us through the woods. It was a raised wooden
20   path that took you through lots of trees and bushes and ...
21   *(Pauses, remembering)* **There** was this smell of ... nature. A
22   smell of moss and dampness, I guess.

23    It was on this path that this thing happened. We were
24   talking and laughing and having fun and I suddenly got this
25   idea. I don't know where it came from. It was like it flew into
26   my head and made me say it. It was like I had no choice. At
27   least I tell myself that now. So, this idea came into my head
28   and when we reached a place where the path went out in

1 several directions. I whispered to the three other girls when
2 Amy was far enough ahead of us that she couldn't hear. I
3 said, "Hey, let's count to three and then run from Amy. We
4 should all run in different directions so she won't know who
5 to follow.

6     For some reason they all said yes. Why they did or what
7 would have happened if they didn't is something I think
8 about everyday. But, it doesn't really matter now I suppose.
9 They said yes and we did and that ... *(Gets very quiet)* is the
10 last time we ever saw Amy.

11     I don't tell many people about it. People here don't know
12 because that happened in Florida and that's exactly why my
13 parents moved to New York. So that no one would know.
14 They won't admit to that. They say it was to be closer to my
15 grandparents, but I know. They didn't want to run into
16 Amy's mom at the grocery store or see her father at the
17 garage. It's not the kind of thing that anyone can forget or
18 ever get over. Amy is missing. And ... it's because of me.

# 19. Scenes from the Tree House

1      What do I remember from the tree house? I remember a
2  lot of things, but like I told you last week, I won't tell you,
3  or anyone, everything that I remember. I made a pact. You
4  said that was OK, remember? "Just tell me what you're
5  ready to tell, Eliza." That's what you said, remember? OK.
6  OK. Just checking.

7      *(Sighs.)* Well, I thought about it all week and I made a
8  little outline in my head. I'm going to give you a beginning,
9  a middle, and an end, just like any good story should have.
10 I'll even give you a little bit of conflict, but not the whole
11 thing. I'll leave the meat out and give you the bones. Bone
12 number one, the beginning. The idea of the tree house
13 started at the beginning of the summer between seventh
14 and eighth grade. Erin's oldest sister was going off to
15 college that summer and getting absolutely all of the
16 attention. She was used to being in the spotlight because
17 she was beautiful and brilliant. Erin was used to being in her
18 shadow, but somehow that summer the shadow had grown
19 even longer than usual and Erin was looking for a way to
20 poke her head out into the sun.

21     We had this little club that we called the Girls Only Club.
22 We'd started it in fifth grade in Mrs. O'Neal's class and had
23 somehow managed to keep it alive for three years. The
24 membership was small, but we were fiercely loyal to one
25 another. Erin, me, Lisa, and Lee. Erin came to our first
26 meeting that summer at Lee's house with a look that said
27 she'd been crying. The second we closed Lee's bedroom
28 door it all just poured out of her. She hated her sister, she

1 needed her own place in the world, etcetera, etcetera. I'm
2 sure you can imagine the kinds of feelings she was going
3 through. We tried to make her feel better by saying, "Look,
4 your sister is going away. She'll get all the attention right
5 now, but after she goes, that will leave more of the spotlight
6 for you." Nothing seemed to make her feel better.
7      Lisa mentioned that we needed to start our meeting
8 because she had to go home in half an hour to baby-sit. So,
9 we put Erin's problem aside and started on the agenda.
10 Every summer, the number one item was building a tree
11 house. It was something that we had wanted to do every
12 year, but every year it didn't happen. This year, the minute
13 Lee read the first item on the agenda, Erin's face lit up.
14 "That's it," she said. "That's it! The tree house will be the
15 one thing that I can have that Rowena never had. She will
16 always be the most beautiful, the most beloved by the
17 grandparents, the smartest, the most popular, but she
18 never had a tree house and now she's grown up and going
19 away and she'll never get to have one for as long as she
20 lives."
21      We all looked at her like she was a bit crazy. Lisa
22 mumbled, "She doesn't need a tree house, she's got a
23 dorm." Lee and I looked at her like we could kill her. Erin
24 just went on, "This summer! This is the summer that we
25 *must* build the tree house. If we don't build the tree house,
26 I have nothing to live for. No reason to be." We should have
27 known that this was crazy talk, but I think we all felt this
28 sort of odd excitement at the urgency that was suddenly
29 being placed on this whim of ours that had been pushed
30 aside every year in favor of reality. Somehow we wanted
31 something to do that summer that meant life or death and
32 Erin had just handed it to us on a silver platter.

# 20. The Interview

1     First of all, let me say that I don't like to give interviews
2 like this.
3     Yes, it's fun getting all this attention, but I don't like the
4 way the things I say come out on the other side sometimes.
5 I know. I can trust you. I love your magazine. OK, let's get
6 started.
7     How do I feel about being a best-selling author at
8 seventeen? Well, *(Sighs)* it's pretty weird. I've gotten to meet
9 so many new people that I would never have even dreamed
10 of meeting. New friends? Well, no, not really new friends.
11 Just people who want to meet me because of the book.
12     How has it affected my old friendships? Not in a good
13 way. It's ... *(Sighs)* ... you see, when I write, it's like I'm
14 creating a collage. I take bits and pieces of real life, images
15 that I've stored in my head, things I've heard people say,
16 and I mix those with the imaginary, the great "what if." But
17 sometimes, people who have been part of my life recognize
18 something of themselves and think that I'm speaking
19 directly about them.
20     For example? Well, to give you an idea, it's like my
21 cousin was Homecoming Queen at her high school and she
22 was in a car accident that night and didn't make the
23 homecoming football game. Well, I use that circumstance in
24 my book, right? But that character, the Homecoming
25 Queen, is nothing like my cousin. I mean, my cousin is
26 nothing like her. My cousin is sweet and smart and not evil
27 in any way. So, I think she was a bit offended by my book
28 because she thought I was making some sort of statement

1   about her, but I'm not. I'm simply borrowing from life and
2   mixing it up with my imagination.
3       Boyfriends? Hmmmm. Well, no. The book hasn't really
4   changed that for me. I was too busy writing before the book
5   was published and now I'm too busy doing all this publicity
6   stuff. With all that and school, I don't have time for a
7   boyfriend. I mean, I do date occasionally, but I can't commit
8   to one boyfriend. They would just be vying for my attention
9   right now and all of my attention has to be on this book right
10  now.
11      My ideal date? Oh, that's easy. Dinner and a movie.
12  Really simple. With whom? Hmmmm. I'd rather not name
13  names. What would he be like? Well, I can tell you that he
14  wouldn't be a vampire. *(Laughs.)* That's not my fantasy, the
15  forbidden love kind of thing, or the bad boy type. No, I'd like
16  someone who is actually going to make my life easier, not
17  more complicated. And I think that's sort of the message
18  that I wanted girls to get out of my book. You know, it's
19  exciting in a story to read about these risky relationships
20  that these characters have, but in real life, it's pretty
21  dangerous. If you know that someone's bad news in any sort
22  of way, I think you shouldn't go there. Stay away and find
23  someone who is all of the good things that you want. That's
24  the message in my book and that's what I hope girls take
25  away from it. Go toward the light. Leave the dark and
26  dangerous to themselves. They deserve each other.

# 21. Black Out

1     I wake up in the night and I can't go back to sleep. I look
2  at the clock. Great. It's just after three a.m. Again. I lie
3  back down for a minute and try to close my eyes. Go back
4  to sleep, go back to sleep. "Slip back in," I tell myself, "or
5  you'll be a zombie again tomorrow." It's beginning to take
6  its toll.
7     But my brain doesn't listen. My eyes pop open and my
8  thoughts start turning. I'm thinking of everything I need to
9  do before second period tomorrow. Everything that I was
10 supposed to do for homework last night. How am I going to
11 fit it all into homeroom? Maybe I should just turn on the
12 lights and do it now. But I'm tired. And I don't want to work.
13 I want to walk.
14    I want to go out the bedroom door and down the hall to
15 the living room. Cross to the front door on my tiptoes so I
16 don't make a sound. Then, I open the door, and I'm free.
17 Out under the stars. It's chilly out here. I'm in my bare feet
18 and my pajamas, but there's no one awake to see. The
19 street is dark and I'm alone. I walk, then I look back for a
20 moment at the house to see if a light has come on. No. No
21 one heard. Good. I'm out in the darkness, in the cold, but
22 I'm free. Free from that house and the things that go on
23 there. Free from the burden of being the daughter, the
24 sister, the high school student with so many things to do.
25    I'm hearing the sounds of the cars whirring by on the
26 nearby highway. My feet are cold and an occasional rock
27 bruises my foot. But I don't care. I'm walking faster now. I
28 decide that I'll walk all the way to the foot of the hill and

1 back. It's not that far, but I've got to turn a corner and I
2 won't be able to look back and see the house. I turn the
3 corner and it seems even darker here. It's such a dark night.
4 I see stars, but the moon has gone behind a cloud. Or I
5 guess a cloud has come in front of it. I stop for a moment
6 and look up. I see my breath in the air. I see the cloud slip
7 away and unveil the moon. "Beautiful," I say to no one.
8 Suddenly I hear a dog barking and I get scared. "This is
9 crazy," I think. My body turns about-face and I start to a run
10 back to the house. The dog barking seems to be getting
11 closer. I start repeating a little prayer out loud and hear
12 myself huffing out the words. I step on a really sharp rock
13 and I stumble a little bit. I stop to massage my foot and
14 catch my breath. I can't run anymore and the dog is getting
15 closer. And now I realize that an alarm is going off. I wake
16 up. I open my eyes to the sunlight.

# 22. And His Name Was Tanner Lawrie

1     I don't talk about it because no one understands. No
2 one. Not even the people that were there. They saw, but
3 they were blind. He was the most wonderful, the most
4 beautiful person. But no one saw. They only saw what he
5 had done as something wrong, something crazy, but he
6 knew. He just knew too much. He's ... his ideas are beyond
7 his years, beyond our time. Oh, of course I'm talking crazy.
8 Go ahead, call me crazy too. Why not! If they'd called him
9 crazy, go ahead and call me that too. I consider it a
10 compliment to be put in the same category as him. Yes, I
11 know it seems like I'm in love with him.
12     You'd like to meet him? I wish that could be arranged.
13 But, who knows where he is right now. I mean, they
14 practically threatened to kill him if he didn't leave town. Oh
15 Jeannie, you should have been there. It was awful. But
16 exciting too, for some strange reason. It was like the
17 universe was on the brink of change. And Jeannie, there are
18 an awful lot of people who don't like change. No matter what
19 it means to them in the end.
20     He said they were frightened and that he understood. He
21 said that the change agents in this world have to be
22 courageous and buck up against the crowd. He said that he
23 didn't mind dedicating his whole life to change if it meant
24 that people would be better off in the end.
25     Oh, yes, Jeannie, he does sound wonderful, because he
26 was. Wonderful. And I feel like I was blessed just to know
27 him for a time. And you're special too Jeannie, because you
28 seem to understand. But I know that I can't expect most

1 people to. To understand, that is, and to appreciate him.
2 That's why I won't tell anyone but you. Is that all right? Will
3 you be my confidante? Whenever I'm thinking about him and
4 I just want to burst? Whenever I'm sitting in school listening
5 to some dry lecture and my eyes well up with tears? Can I
6 come and confide in you again? Oh, thank you, Jeannie. I
7 wish you could have been there. But being there for me is
8 so kind of you.

9 Oh Jeannie, if you had only known him. He was tall and
10 strong. He was kind and gentle. And his ideas. Oh Jeannie,
11 his ideas. They were so far beyond our time. He was a
12 genius. Not like those kids you see with their nose in a book
13 in the library, but a genius with his head in the stars. Yes, I
14 met the most wonderful man that I'll meet in my life. And
15 his name was Tanner Lawrie.

# 23. Monologues for Moynihan

1     I tell you, I won't do it! I will not do a monologue for
2 Moynihan Foster's birthday. She is not my friend! I unfriend
3 her.
4     *(Sighs.)* Mother, you just don't get it, do you? Moynihan
5 Foster gets everything. She has always gotten everything, or
6 if not everything at least always something better than me.
7 And I've put up with it for all these years, but this is too
8 much. *(Picks up an invitation and reads.)* **"You are cordially**
9 **invited to Monologues for Moynihan, a special evening of**
10 **performance in honor of Moynihan Foster's sixteenth**
11 **birthday."** You must have told her mother what you're
12 getting me for my birthday, right? And she just had to outdo
13 you. I thought for once I'd have one up on Moynihan. But no!
14     Oh, come on, Mother, don't pretend you don't know
15 what I'm talking about. You know this whole competition
16 thing started from the day we were born. The day you had
17 me is the day that you met Moynihan's mother. The two of
18 you in the hospital, sharing a room. Both of you the proud
19 parents of two baby girls. You and Daddy were free spirits
20 and you wanted to give me a name that was different and
21 special. And you tried, you really did. Brooke. It's pretty at
22 least, if not too unique. But Moynihan's mother just had to
23 top you. She gave her little perfect Moynihan the most
24 unique name anyone's probably ever heard. And every year
25 at Moynihan's birthday party her mom gives a teary-eyed
26 speech about the reason she named her Moynihan is so that
27 she'd have a name as unique and special as she is. And
28 every year at her party, the other five Brookes and I have to

1  sit there and politely listen.

2     But Mother, this year, this year is the topper of all
3  toppers. This even beats the year that you finally let me
4  have a pet — a *jumping bean! And Moynihan Foster got a*
5  *pony!* I'm sorry, Mother. I really am. I'm sorry for raising my
6  voice. I know it's disrespectful and I don't mean to be. It's
7  just, you must understand. I cannot, I will not contribute to
8  an evening of monologues about Moynihan Foster if it's the
9  last thing I do. I will not stand in that spotlight and celebrate
10 her birthday or celebrate our friendship, or announce her
11 unusual name to the world. I just won't do it, Mother. I will
12 not do a monologue for Moynihan Foster.

# 24. Thick-Skinned

1     I'm supposed to be thick-skinned. Doesn't that sound
2 gross? Thick-skinned. That's what Mother always calls me.
3 "Andrea can take anything. She's so thick-skinned." All my
4 life, kids could call me names and I'd never flinch. Now,
5 Dorie, my sister, she would cry like a baby and run to her
6 mama, but not me. I'd just threaten to kick someone's butt.
7     But does that mean that I don't have feelings? Does that
8 mean all those words didn't hurt? Of course not! But you
9 know what, that's what everyone thinks. I'm "thick-
10 skinned." Nothing bothers me. Well, you know what, I've got
11 a news flash for them. Everything bothers me. I just don't
12 show it. I'm like the world's best poker player when it comes
13 to feelings. You'll never know what I'm thinking or what I'm
14 feeling. No, everyone's careful with Dorie. "Be sweet to
15 Dorie. She's soooo sensitive." Well, hey, you know what, I've
16 got news for you. *I'm sensitive, for crying out loud!*
17     *(Looks down shaking head.)* I don't know why I'm telling
18 you this. I guess I've heard those two words just one time
19 too many. Thick-skinned. Thick-skinned. Thick-skinned.
20 Yeah, I heard Mother on the phone last night talking about
21 the things that people are saying about her and my dad.
22 "I'm not worried about Andrea," she says. "Andrea can take
23 anything. She's so thick-skinned." Then she says, "It's
24 Dorie I'm worried about. She's so easily shattered." So, she
25 doesn't worry about me. Nice. 'Cause I've been tough and
26 haven't whined every time somebody stepped on my toes.
27 *(Sighs.)* I get no sympathy and no concern whatsoever.
28 Mother! My own mother! How can she be so blind? How can

1 she be so cold? I tell you what, I've got news for you.
2 *(Shakes head.)* If I could do it all again, I'd be the
3 thinnest-skinned girl in this town. If I could go back to ...
4 *(Thinking)* OK, first grade for instance. When David Pazinski
5 called me ugly, I'd have bawled my eyes out instead of
6 socking him in the jaw. And in fourth grade, when
7 everybody, including the teacher, accused me of stealing the
8 class turtle — falsely accused me, I might add — well, I
9 would have run home to my mama all teary-eyed and told
10 her that I could never set foot in that classroom again.
11 Instead, I said, "Yeah, I stole Turtle Tom and I ate him for
12 *lunch!*" I made at least five kids cry. It was hilarious. And
13 did they say they were sorry when they found out that Joey
14 Hester stole the turtle? Heck no! Why should they? I don't
15 have any feelings. Don't you know that? *(Sighs.)* Yeah, if I
16 could do it all over again, I'd have skin as thin as ... I don't
17 know, Dorie's I guess. Yeah, I'd be just like Dorie.

# 25. The Swap Shop

1    Last year, just before school started, we were really
2  short of money. We were at the end of our rope is another
3  way of putting it I guess. I don't know how it happened, but
4  my family is not the luckiest when it comes to finances, if
5  you know what I mean. Money comes in slowly and goes out
6  quickly. My dad gets a bonus, my mom's car goes in the
7  shop. My mom wins at Bingo and my dad gets fired. It's like
8  there's this law in our house that says what comes in must
9  go out and take some extra money with it.
10    So, anyway, I'm getting off track. As I was saying, last
11  year, just before school started, we were desperate for cash.
12  Mom's credit cards were maxed out and all of my money
13  from baby-sitting, washing cars, and stuff had been eaten
14  up by stupid summer stuff. You know, movies, pizza, stuff I
15  probably could have done without, I'm sure. Only I would
16  have died of boredom. Well, anyway, I'd spent my money.
17  Mom spent her money on credit card bills and Dad spent his
18  money on gas and stuff, out there pounding the pavement
19  trying to look for work. So, I wanted new clothes for school,
20  Mom wanted to pay some extra bills that popped up, and
21  there we were. So, we decided to get rid of some junk and
22  make a little extra cash at the same time. And we thought,
23  "Hey, the best way to do that is at the swap shop, right?"
24    I thought the whole idea was kind of cool at first, but
25  getting up at like four in the morning to get ready was not
26  so cool. It was painful. Then, piling everything into the car
27  wasn't easy either. You can only fit so much in that car and
28  still be able to sit in it. And I had decided that I would sell

1   just about everything I owned in order to get some cool
2   clothes for school. Mom kept saying stuff like, "Awe, do you
3   really want to sell Stinky Bear?" And I'd be like, "Yes, *Mom.*
4   This is no time for sentimentality! I need some clothes!"
5   She kind of kept wiping a tear from her eye when she'd see
6   me stick something else in the car. She'd start to say
7   something to stop me and I'd be like, "Don't."
8      It was kind of funny, now that I look back. 'Cause she
9   didn't have to worry, really. I mean, as it turns out, nobody
10  at the swap shop wanted to buy Stinky Bear anyway. At
11  least, not for what I was asking. Well, you know, I can sell
12  my stuff, but I can't sell it for nothing. It's important stuff
13  ... to me. And Stinky Bear for a quarter? I don't think so.
14  Well, anyway, we ended up sweating it out in that hot sun
15  all day for about twenty-five bucks. At the end of the day we
16  had to pack everything in the car, *again.* And it was even
17  harder because my mom bought a baby carriage for five
18  bucks from some lady that she felt sorry for. I'm like, "Mom.
19  A baby carriage? Is there something I should know?" She
20  just rolled her eyes at me and said, "I just felt so sorry for
21  her. She looked so down on her luck." I just shook my
22  head. I mean, I guess she was right. As broke as we were,
23  we still weren't down on our luck. I mean, hey, we had each
24  other. And, better yet, we still had Stinky Bear. How bad
25  could things be?

# 26. Downsized

1  My parents recently decided to downsize prior to their
2  annual European vacation. I'm not being facetious. It's
3  completely true. Oh, of course they'd deny it, but I
4  happened to overhear them just before the actual event
5  took place. The day, that is, that they let me go, laid me off,
6  made me a victim of downsizing, or whatever you'd like to
7  call it.
8  You see, it was a Saturday and I was in the throes of
9  trying to write my autobiography. It's something that I've
10 always felt compelled to do. Just intuition I guess, but I've
11 always known that I will do great things one day, so I want
12 to be ready for the moment, so to speak. But, be that as it
13 may, I was, as I said, in the throes of writing my
14 autobiography and I wanted to find some intriguing
15 information about my parents that hadn't been previously
16 disclosed. I knew that my mother had a diary from her
17 college years and I wanted to get some valid information
18 about how my parents met. Of course they had told the fairy
19 tale of love at first sight and whirling down the aisle to
20 eternal bliss, but I wanted to know if there was any dirt. It's
21 important to know your own family dirt before you publish
22 an autobiography. If there's anything to tell, you should
23 definitely be the first to tell it. The media has a field day with
24 people who try to hide their dirty laundry.
25 Anyway, I digress. So, I go to my parent's bedroom and
26 I find my mother's diary, but just as I begin to turn the
27 pages, I hear them coming. Not wanting to get caught, I did
28 what any mature young woman would do. I hid under the

1 bed. Yes, I know it's a disgusting thing to do, what with all
2 the dust bunnies, wads of tissues, and old socks one finds
3 under there. But, be that as it may, I hid under the bed and
4 that's when I heard them talking. They said that with the
5 economy and its impact on our family business, they might
6 have to make some changes to the European vacation this
7 year. At first they talked about making it shorter, but
8 Mother just couldn't see doing London in less than ten
9 days. Then, Father mentioned the possibility of a less
10 expensive hotel. At that, I think I heard my mother sob. But
11 her despair was brief, for she suddenly had a brilliant
12 revelation.
13     She said that she really didn't think a teenager of my
14 age truly wanted to spend the summer with her parents. My
15 father quite agreed, adding quickly that his sister Betsy
16 would be all alone for the summer with her husband away in
17 the service and she could most certainly use some
18 company.
19     So, within the space of ten minutes, perhaps less, I was
20 eliminated from the trip, thus, as you can imagine, reducing
21 expenses considerably. My sister Delilah was left on the trip
22 roster, of course. She's only eight, so I suppose she's safe
23 for a couple more years, but eventually she'll be shipped off
24 to some other place as well.
25     So, I've been at Aunt Betsy's for almost six weeks now.
26 My mother wrote once and said that they're having a
27 marvelous time. And I'm glad. I don't mind that the family
28 downsized for the trip, really I don't. I just hope I still have
29 a bedroom when I get back home. And I haven't minded
30 spending the summer with Aunt Betsy one bit. She can be
31 quite amusing, actually. And she and I have quite a few
32 things in common. Well, for one thing, we both think my
33 mother's diary is an absolute hoot.

# 27. A Summer Story

1    How can I tell him? Why doesn't he understand? I ...
2  Things are not the same during summer. Summer ends and
3  things go back to normal and you're not supposed to expect
4  somebody to be who they were, do the things that they did,
5  for a few short months playing by the shore.
6    *(Sighs.)* What am I talking about? Oh, don't you know?
7  Remember that boy that I told you I met this summer.
8  *(Looks down.)* Yes, the wonderful one. No, well, yes, I said I
9  was in love, but that's just what I'm trying to explain. A girl
10 can say she's in love, even believe she's in love, in the
11 summer. But that girl that was in love goes away when the
12 fall comes around and a new girl takes her place. I came
13 back home and started my real life back up again very
14 nicely. I'm somebody in this town. I'm not the girl picking up
15 shells every morning on the beach. I have plans. I have
16 friends. Friends who have plans. Like Harvard and Yale. He's
17 ... his family moves from town to town selling things. Oh, I
18 don't know, stupid things like gadgets that help you
19 organize your tool shed or clean up your kitchen.
20    Oh, he was wonderful, he really was. In the summer! But
21 I never planned to see him again. I never thought that on the
22 first day of school he'd be the first person that I bumped
23 into in the hall. It was terrible. I wanted to be happy to see
24 him, but I was mortified. People were watching. John was
25 watching. And you know that John and I have got to go to
26 the homecoming dance this year. I've been dreaming about
27 it for years. Even our parents have been dreaming about it
28 for years. And here's this guy in torn up sneakers with an

1 old worn out book bag, looking at me as if I'm supposed to
2 jump in his arms and kiss him. Oh, I mean some part of me
3 did want to kiss him. But I brushed that part of me aside. I
4 said, "Hello, nice to see you again." Then I walked right by
5 him and rushed up to John. We walked away as I asked him
6 about the summer.
7     No. I didn't even look back. And that's what I'm
8 supposed to do, what I have a right to do. That's what
9 summer is for. You have fun being the somebody that you
10 can't be all year and if you don't want to, you don't even
11 have to look back. How could this happen to me? What's he
12 done? Nothing. Except for spoil everything. I mean, I can
13 ignore him and go on and go out with John and be the
14 Homecoming Queen. Oh, well, you know I will be. But it
15 spoils everything knowing he's here and knowing how I'm
16 treating him. I do have a conscience you know. I do have a
17 heart. Oh, I wish he would just go away.

# 28. The Girl Next Door

1   When I was in middle school there was this girl next door
2   that I avoided like the plague. The best way to describe her
3   is ... well, let's see, she was kind of like a pit bull. Not just
4   any pit bull, but you know that one that was recently in the
5   news for mauling its owner? That pit bull. Yes, that's the one
6   that reminds me of her. Even my parents were afraid of her.
7   They'd never admit to it, but I'm pretty sure she's the
8   reason my dad put up that fence that was ten feet high with
9   barbed wire on top. That made it pretty easy to avoid her at
10  home, but at school that was a different story.
11      One day, I was in the lunch line at River Middle and I felt
12  someone's eyes on me. I didn't want to look, but it was so
13  hard not to. You know how that is, right? It's like this weird
14  feeling you get when you feel someone's evil eyes burrowing
15  into you like a flame from the burning pit below. Well, that's
16  exactly the feeling I got that day and so my eye glanced over
17  to see what it was. And sure enough there *she* was, the pit
18  bull, staring right at me. I felt my flesh go numb and my
19  eyes grow wide. I started to turn away, but before I could,
20  she spoke. Somewhere from the depths of the vacuum
21  where a soul should have been, she growled. "What are you
22  looking at?" I squeaked out, "Nothing." My voice sounded
23  foreign, even to my own ears. It was like ... like it came from
24  a little mouse that had been stepped on by someone's big
25  foot. She glared at me like she wanted to destroy me and I
26  turned away. I was glad we were in the cafeteria and not in
27  some hallway with no one else there.
28      But later that afternoon, that's exactly what happened.

1 I was in Mrs. Rollaway's class doing an assignment in our
2 grammar books and she suddenly said that she needed
3 someone to take something to the office for her. I tried to
4 keep my eyes glued to my book. I knew that there must be
5 twenty hands raised who were anxious to go, but she
6 wouldn't let them. She knew that they just didn't want to
7 decide which was the subject and which was the predicate
8 and what was a dangling participle and all that. No, Mrs.
9 Rollaway wanted someone to go who didn't want to go.
10 "Melissa," she called out. I pretended to be so engrossed
11 with my work that I didn't hear, but she said it louder, more
12 insistently, "Melissa!"
13   "Yes, Mrs. Rollaway," I said.
14   "Melissa, take this envelope to the front office, please,
15 and give it to Mrs. Dixon."
16   "Yes, Mrs. Rollaway."
17   I left the room with the little brown envelope in my hand.
18 The halls were extremely dark that day because it was about
19 to storm. There was thunder and darkness and not a soul in
20 sight. As I walked down the hall I passed the girls'
21 restroom. Someone came out, and as the door opened I saw
22 a swirl of cigarette smoke out of the corner of my eye. I kept
23 walking, but a moment later I heard the restroom door
24 squeak open again and the footsteps that came afterward
25 started trailing behind me. I wanted to look back, but I knew
26 that I shouldn't. I started walking a little faster and the
27 footsteps started getting faster. I started running and the
28 footsteps started running. It was her. I knew it was her.
29   I felt her hand on my arm. I turned and was prepared to
30 scream "Let go of me!" But before I did I saw what was in
31 her hand. "You dropped this in the hall," she said. She
32 handed the little brown envelope to me, looked embarrassed
33 by her kindness, and quickly added "Idiot." She turned and
34 was gone in a flash.

# 29. The Divorce

1     So, was it messy? Your parents' divorce? Oh, that's
2 good. Believe me, "not too messy" is much better than *very*
3 messy. Oh yes. Ours was *very* messy. Well, yes, my
4 parents', but I say "ours" because it really was a family
5 affair, you know. My parents dragged us into it from the
6 moment the ball started rolling. I mean, they had always
7 dragged us into everything anyway. The fights, the
8 accusations. We were always being asked, or should I say
9 forced, to take sides. And there were so many events in our
10 lives, events that should have been happy, but just couldn't
11 be. The tension, you know, it was always present. *(Sighs.)*
12 So, why should the divorce have been any different?
13     Well, I always knew that Mother would win out in the
14 end. She fought the hardest and the dirtiest. She was
15 always the one who wore the pants in our house, you know.
16 I mean, I used to feel sorry for my dad, actually. And I never,
17 in a million years, thought that I'd be the one helping her to
18 destroy Dad. But, life is ironic, you know. Yes, eventually I
19 joined a side and it was Mother's, fully and one hundred
20 percent. Finally, after years of trying to stay neutral, of
21 trying to mitigate and mediate, trying to be the peacemaker.
22 I mean, I, as most children do, loved both of my parents.
23     What happened to make me turn against Dad? It was
24 really a little thing. In fact, if I were an objective observer,
25 I'm quite certain that I could say it was the smallest, most
26 insignificant thing that you could imagine and that my
27 reaction to it was an emotionally immature and purely
28 childish one. But, what can I say, what happened ...

1   happened. And the way I felt and what I did was ... just
2   that, the way I felt and what I did. Que sera, sera, you know.
3   What will be, will be. Sometimes, we just can't help being
4   who we are, feeling what we feel, and our reactions, you
5   know, they are what they are. What happened? Yes, I'll tell
6   you what happened.
7       You see, my mother and father separated at some point.
8   After this separation had been going for about a year, my
9   father began seeing another woman. He said that she was
10 only a friend, but my mother was furious. I wasn't happy
11 about it either, because I knew it meant that they would
12 probably really and truly never get back together again and
13 that this time our family would really never be a family
14 again. But I think I still had some hope and why I even
15 wanted to hope for that, I don't know. I suppose that's
16 another story.
17      So, anyway, one evening, my mother decided to cheer us
18 up, I guess. She knew that I loved the theatre, so she
19 bought tickets to a show that I'd been dying to see. We
20 couldn't afford the best seats, but she got us two seats in
21 the nosebleed section and we took our binoculars. I was so
22 excited just to be in the theatre. Before the show began I
23 took the binoculars and looked at all the beautiful people
24 down below in the orchestra section — couples dressed to
25 the nines and families so happy together.
26      I remember that there was a mother and daughter in
27 beautiful matching black velvet gowns. And then, I saw him.
28 My father. At first I was happy to see him. But I felt a pang
29 of fear that he and my mother might run into each other and
30 that would most definitely spoil the night. Especially
31 because he had a beautiful blonde woman on his arm. That
32 made me worried and sad, but what I saw next made me
33 even sadder. It wasn't just a beautiful blonde woman that
34 he had with him. He was with her beautiful blonde daughter
35 and son as well. There they were. All happy together. They

1 were smiling and laughing like one happy family. My dad
2 even put his arm around the girl's shoulder at one point as
3 he led them to their lovely expensive seats in the center of
4 the orchestra, about the fifth row. I put the binoculars down.
5 I couldn't look anymore.
6     And I don't remember anything about the show that
7 night. I just know that after that night, I disowned my father
8 in my mind. I was completely on my mother's side
9 throughout the whole divorce. And it got very messy, believe
10 me. I even had to testify in court. Against my father. But ...
11 I did it. I never thought I would. But ... that night in the
12 theatre, you know, something inside me ... it just died.

# 30. The Color of Love

1     Darren asks me what my favorite color is. He knows that
2 this is not a simple question for me, a painter. He smiles
3 and I think aloud. "My favorite color?" He nods. He sees the
4 weight of the question on my face and he is amused.

5     "My favorite color ... " I begin, but I am thinking. I close
6 my eyes and in my head there is a kaleidoscope presenting
7 me with memories in the form of color. I see my paintings.
8 I see many paintings and in those paintings I see the
9 moments. I remember the moments. I see magenta, for the
10 painting of the old house, I remember the magenta. There
11 was a moment when magenta was the answer and the truth.
12 The truth of the old house. Then, I see a puddle of burnt
13 sienna. There was a time when it was burnt sienna.

14     But then, Granddad, the painting of Granddad comes
15 into my head. His sweater was maroon, but flecked with tiny
16 golden pieces. I remember how I wanted, I needed, to
17 capture Granddad's sweater with exactly the right color.
18 Especially after he was gone. I wanted something to keep
19 him alive. I wanted to remember the time in my life when he
20 came to me and picked me up and swung me around. I
21 wanted to have a memory, a vivid memory, of my life as an
22 artist when all that I knew were the primary colors.

23     *(Smiles.)* Yes, primary colors and there is green, swirling
24 green everywhere. *(Laughs.)* My finger painting in Ms. Bell's
25 class. It is the most beautiful green swirling finger painting
26 that anyone has ever seen and I bring it home and we name
27 it "Snakes." It takes its place on the gallery wall that we call
28 "The Fridge." And I am now being called, *(With grandeur)*

1   "The artist in the family."

2      The sound of Darren's footsteps brings me back into the

3   room. I see him walking around the studio, looking at my

4   paintings, looking at my palette and my twisted and tired oil

5   paints, my old, dried up watercolors. The stains on the floor.

6   So many colors. But my favorite color? My favorite color, my

7   favorite color ... my eyes close again, and now I'm seeing a

8   movie and it is my life. My life in primary colors. It is a white

9   room and I am in a small bed. My mother walks in wearing

10  a pink dress. I cry. She comes to me and holds me. I am not

11  well and she is comforting me. She wipes my tears and

12  holds me, rocking me against her pink dress. I look up into

13  her face. It is a beautiful face. I am looking into her face and

14  she is smiling and singing and telling me stories and I feel

15  loved.

16      I look into her face and I am mesmerized by her eyes.

17  Her beautiful blue eyes and I am wondering why my eyes are

18  brown. She tells me I have my daddy's eyes and that I am

19  going to be beautiful one day. I will have my daddy's brown

20  eyes and her red hair and I will be the only one of me in the

21  entire world. Did she know those would be her last words to

22  me? I have always wondered. It is my last memory of her and

23  I have played it in my head a million times. In my memory I

24  see a sadness in her eyes that must have been a knowing,

25  a sense that she would have to part.

26      I hear Darren's footsteps moving toward me and I open

27  my eyes to see him reaching for my hand. He touches my

28  face and looks down at me. "Have you decided?" He

29  twinkles with the mirth of the occasion, but then he sees the

30  tear roll down my face and he looks puzzled. "Yes," I say. "I

31  don't know why I had to think at all. It is blue. My favorite

32  color is blue."

# 31. Talking to Myself

1      I talk to myself. That's how I get through the day. You
2  should try it. I mean, not out loud or anything, unless I'm,
3  like, all alone in my room or something. Or, like, in the
4  bathroom, I'll talk to myself in the bathroom mirror. But I
5  also do it all day, at school and stuff, in my head, ya know.
6      That's how I survive it, the mess that my life is right
7  now. Well, I say "right now," but it's pretty much always
8  been that way. A mess. But I talk to myself and I tell myself
9  that it won't always be this way. And that's why I should
10  keep going. That's why I should keep putting one foot in
11  front of the other and just keep, ya know, being there. Yeah,
12  being there. Like, ya know, being at this school even though
13  I have no friends. I know, I know, I could try to make friends,
14  but it's hard. I have moved to a new school almost every
15  year of my life and this year, I feel like I've landed in this
16  alien place where I just don't fit in at all. Well, for one thing,
17  I'm not rich like most of the kids here. My mom can barely
18  pay our rent most months. I don't wear the nicest clothes in
19  the world. I try to work with what I have. I go to thrift stores
20  and I try to think of my stuff as vintage, ya know. And I tell
21  myself, "One day, you'll have better clothes, but if people
22  don't like you or want to get to know you because you're not
23  dressed the way they think you should be, then you don't
24  want to know them anyway."
25      But it's hard. It is. Sometimes when I tell myself things
26  like that I look back at myself in the mirror and I'm like,
27  "You're lying. I do want to know them. I want them to like
28  me. I am like everyone else. I want to feel liked. Even loved.

1    And *you* are a big fat liar. I hate you." That's a really bad
2    day, when I'm like that. I'll get so mad at myself that I won't
3    even talk to myself anymore. But I always get over it.
4    Eventually. And then I'm right back at it again, telling myself
5    to hang in there. Telling myself it will all be great one day
6    and I'll look back on all this loneliness, all this despair, and
7    I'll laugh. I'll be like, "I told you so."

# 32. The Women

1       There are so many amazing and interesting women in
2 the history of the United States that you should know. Can
3 I introduce them to you? Not personally, like you won't get
4 to shake their hand or anything. But I can tell you about
5 them. In some cases, I can show you their work. My
6 favorites are right here in this room. Like, well, look, here's
7 a book. It's a collection of poetry by Dorothy Parker. She
8 was so cool, so funny, so cynical. I think she was wonderful.
9 And, *(Looks around the room)* and here's a little print I bought
10 last summer at the museum when my family and I went to
11 New York. It's a Georgia O'Keefe. Isn't that just the coolest
12 flower that you've ever seen? Or how about Mary Walton? My
13 mom gave me this book about women inventors and it tells
14 how she was one of the pioneers in the fight against
15 pollution. She developed a method for minimizing the
16 environmental hazards of the smoke that was pouring from
17 factories all over the country. She got a patent for her
18 system back in the late 1800s.
19       And you know what's really amazing? These great
20 women, women like Mary Walton, Dorothy Parker, Georgia
21 O'Keefe, they were born many years before women even had
22 the right to vote in the United States. Yes, really. Dorothy
23 Parker, for instance, was born in 1893. Georgia O'Keefe was
24 born in 1887. So, they both were young women when the
25 right to vote was finally bestowed on the female sex. Yes,
26 that's right. The nineteenth amendment to the constitution
27 was signed into law in August of 1920, granting women the
28 right to vote. That's right, it didn't happen until 1920, just
29 after World War I.

1   So, let's see, *(Doing the math in her head)* **Dorothy would**
2   have been twenty-seven and Georgia O'Keefe thirty-three.
3   And they had some great women to thank for that right, too.
4   Yeah, like Elizabeth Cady Stanton and Susan B. Anthony.
5   You've never heard of them? Well, you should look them up
6   some time. They were all about women's rights, but you
7   know what, they didn't even get to see the day that women
8   got the right to vote here in the US. No. Elizabeth Cady
9   Stanton died in 1902 and Susan B. Anthony died at the age
10  of eighty-six in 1906. So, most of the work they did was for
11  women who would come after them, who they would never
12  even meet. That's so cool.
13      And there were lots of other women, of course. Women
14  who lived in their time and long after. And the work ... the
15  work that these women did lives on to this day. I mean,
16  when I turn eighteen and I get a chance to vote, I am going
17  to think of them. I will. I don't want to be like most people
18  who just take the right for granted. I mean, we feel like, "Of
19  course we have the right to vote; why wouldn't we?" But, in
20  reality, our predecessors had to fight for it. And imagine
21  what it would be like if we didn't have the right. Well, we're
22  too young to vote right now, but like, let's say at school, we
23  had Student Council elections and only the guys were
24  allowed to vote. We would be furious. We'd fight for the right
25  to have our say. And then, maybe five or ten years later,
26  we'd know that girls at our school had a right that we fought
27  for. We'd expect them to at least realize it, think about it, ya
28  know. That's what I want to do. When I'm eighteen and I
29  walk up to that voting booth, I want to take a moment to
30  think about the women. The women who used their time and
31  energy and intelligence to make things better for me and
32  you. To make things right. That's who I'm going to be
33  thankful for. The women.

# 33. The Experiment

1     Six months ago, I was sitting in the cafeteria having
2  lunch with my friends. We were a pretty close group, my
3  friends and I. Even our parents were, like, best friends. They
4  used to say we were "peas in a pod," "the achievers." Yeah,
5  they used to kind of lump us together like that. And it's
6  true, we were all pretty much in the same place, I mean,
7  academically doing great, always getting recognized for our
8  "excellence," getting elected for things, like Student
9  Council. You know, we were all on the same track. Well,
10  that's what gave Candace the idea. *(Shaking her head)* Yep,
11  the idea. *(Sighs.)* So, yeah, we were all sitting there about
12  six months ago, having lunch, and Candace comes in all
13  excited. "I've got it," she says. "I've got the greatest idea for
14  this year's science project." Well, I know this statement
15  wouldn't be the biggest, most exciting thing to most
16  teenagers, but to our little lunch bunch this was big news.
17  Every year we all dreamed about winning the science
18  project. It was one of the few prizes that had somehow
19  eluded us. So, needless to say, we were all ears.

20  So Candace goes on, "You know how everyone is always
21  talking about positive affirmations and how they can change
22  your life?" I remember looking around the cafeteria at some
23  of the negative kids and I was like "Everyone?" She looked
24  around for a minute and then says, "Well, I mean, you know,
25  everyone who's anyone. Like, in all these self-help books our
26  mothers are reading and those videos that Mrs. Sherman
27  showed us in class last year about visualizing and self-talk
28  and all that positive self-image stuff." So, everyone at the

1    table was like, "Yeah, get to the point. What does this have
2    to do with the science project?"
3       And that was when she explained it all. She had this
4    fantastic idea to use six rather homogeneous volunteers.
5    That would be everyone in our little lunch bunch at the table,
6    of course. She made a point of noting that you couldn't find
7    a more homogeneous group than us. We were all equally
8    smart, extremely confident, and brought up in what we
9    considered to be very good households, with good manners
10   and morals and all that. So, anyway, she went on to say that
11   she wanted to do a study of six homogeneous volunteers
12   over a period of six weeks. The focus of the study would be
13   the impact of positive self-affirmations on the life of a
14   teenage girl. The plan was that two of the volunteers would
15   do a series of positive self-affirmations every day, such as "I
16   am very smart. I am well liked. I am responsible." Stuff like
17   that. Two of the volunteers would do negative affirmations,
18   like "I am an idiot. Nobody likes me. I never get anything
19   accomplished." You get the idea. Oh, and of course, two
20   volunteers would do no affirmations at all. Sort of like a
21   control group, so to speak.
22       So anyway, we all had to admit that this was a pretty
23   cool idea. I mean, I had always wondered if affirmations
24   worked and this seemed like a pretty good way to find out.
25   I was in. We were all in. We went over to Candace's house
26   that night to help her decide on the factors that she would
27   track in all the volunteer's lives. We decided on stuff like
28   grade point average, attendance at school, parent and
29   teacher observations, and special recognition. It seemed
30   pretty easy to determine how a person's life was going if
31   Candace kept track of these simple things. So, the next
32   thing was to decide on who'd be doing negative and who'd
33   be doing positive affirmations. Dara said that she *really*
34   *wanted* to do the positive affirmations. And Linda, who acts
35   like she's Dara's clone, of course had to do them too. I

1 didn't really care if I did positive or negative, but I just knew
2 I didn't want to be the control who did nothing. That
3 obviously seemed like the most boring role. So, I signed up
4 for the "negative team," that would be me and Joanne.
5 Candace sent us all home to get started. We agreed to do
6 our affirmations three times a day for three minutes each
7 time, starting the very next morning.

8 This seemed easy enough, so off I went, going home to
9 set my alarm to wake up just a bit earlier, in order to do my
10 first set of negatives. I was excited, ya know? So, the next
11 morning it started and I did it for three weeks in a very
12 disciplined manner. But then after three weeks, it was
13 weird, I sort of started to slack off. In fact, I sort of started
14 to slack off in a lot of ways, like in English, in math, and
15 even at home. My mother was like, "Since when do you get
16 up from the table and not clear your plate?" And I was like,
17 "Since I don't feel like it anymore." And I went to my room
18 and slammed the door. That's when I knew that something
19 was wrong. That night I could hear my mother crying in the
20 next room, telling my dad that she just didn't know what
21 was going on with me. Candace called me that night too, to
22 get the report on my "particulars." She was like, "What's
23 your average in English?" I said, "I don't know." She was
24 like, "Haha, very funny." I just sat there in silence. She was
25 like, "Marion, are you OK?" I said, "Yeah, but listen, I don't
26 want to do this thing anymore." She was like, "You're
27 kidding, right? That would throw the whole thing off. That
28 would totally invalidate the experiment! You made an
29 agreement. You have to keep your promise." That's when I
30 said, "No, Candace, I don't. I never keep my promises. I am
31 irresponsible. I am dishonest. I never do anything that I say
32 that I'll do!" And then I added before I hung up, "And *you*
33 *are an idiot!*"

34 That was the last time that I talked to Candace. In fact,
35 that's about the last time I talked to anyone in the little

1  "achiever" group. In fact, I didn't even go to school much
2  after that. I would act like I was walking to the bus and then
3  I'd go around the corner and just hang out different places
4  all day. I met some people that I'd never met before and we
5  started having fun and ... *(Trails off)* That's how I ended up
6  here. In juvie. And it's not what I ever expected would
7  happen to me, but it's been a really good thing because I
8  needed time to think. Yeah, I've been thinking a lot. Like, all
9  day long. And I know now that what happened to me was a
10 direct result of that stupid experiment. *(Sighs and shakes her*
11 *head.)* My mom came to visit me the other day. She told me
12 that Candace won the science fair this year. Yep. She won
13 at school; she won in the district; and she won at state. It
14 was a clean sweep. Mom says that Candace gave a speech
15 and said that she really owed it all to me, that this whole
16 juvie thing was, like, the real clincher. *(Sarcastically)* Well,
17 *gee Candace,* so glad I could help. Ya know? So, now, I am
18 trying to turn my life around. Again. But this time I am
19 turning it in the right direction. Every day I do them. My
20 positive affirmations. I say, "I am confident. I am
21 responsible. I am smart." But the one I like best is the one
22 that I hope I will never forget. *"I am not a guinea pig!"*

# 34. 48 States in 52 Weeks

1    My mother is a travel writer. Cool, right? Yeah, pretty
2    cool. Most of the time. But in the past ten years, there's
3    been a lot of weeks when she wasn't home. I mean she
4    travels, right? That's what she does. Unfortunately for me,
5    not being home kind of goes with the territory. But
6    sometimes in the summer I've gotten to go with her. In fact,
7    when I was ten she took me to Paris. That was really cool.
8    And when the article came out about that trip, my picture
9    was in the magazine. Yeah, they put a picture of me in there,
10   sitting at a sidewalk café, stuffing a pastry in my mouth.
11   That was so cool! Of course, none of the kids at school saw
12   it. They weren't into reading the *Traveler* magazine at the
13   time. But I thought it was cool and my mom and I had a
14   great time that summer in Paris.
15       Last year was a little bit different though. My mom got
16   this brilliant idea to do a series of articles chronicling the
17   travels of a single woman crossing the Continental US by
18   car in one year. She decided to call the series "48 States in
19   52 Weeks." Her publisher went absolutely mad for it. So,
20   one night at dinner she broke the news to me. She was
21   giving me an option. I was all grown up now, going into tenth
22   grade. I could go live with my dad for a year or she'd arrange
23   for me to stay with friends while she was away.
24       Now, it might sound like that's an easy decision, but my
25   dad lives about a million miles away. I'd have to change
26   schools and I'd have to get used to his new live-in girlfriend,
27   Tiffany. Now, on the other hand, I had quite a few friends
28   whose parents would probably let me stay with them for a

1   while and my mom had a lot of friends that would let me
2   stay with them for a while too, and some of them weren't all
3   that bad. They lived in our area at least, and they'd take me
4   to school if I needed them to. But Mom made it clear that
5   she wouldn't want to ask anyone to have me for more than
6   a week. That would be imposing and she wouldn't do that.
7   So, I would kind of be nomadic for a year. Sort of like my
8   mom, but in a different way.
9      I told her I'd need a day or two to think about it. I was a
10 little bit scared. Mom had been away a lot and I'd stayed
11 with friends before, but not for such a long stretch. I decided
12 that I'd beg her to take me with her. And I did. But she
13 wouldn't have it. She said it would disrupt my education at
14 a very crucial period in my pre-college existence. Or
15 something like that. I think I cried. Well, no, I know I cried.
16 Sounds dumb, right? But I cried for a really long time that
17 night. I would say that I cried myself to sleep, but I couldn't
18 go to sleep that night, and I took out my journal and
19 decided to write it all out. You know, "I hate my mother,
20 blah, blah, blah. Here's what she's doing to me now, blah,
21 blah, blah."
22      And then, suddenly I got an idea. What if I kept a journal
23 while she was away? Not just any journal of course, but a
24 journal of my experiences in all these different houses that
25 she was arranging for me to stay in. I could write an article
26 about my experiences, or better yet, a book! So, I went in to
27 her bedroom and woke her up. She thought I was crazy, but
28 I said, "When do you leave?"
29      She was like, "What?"
30      I said, "When do you leave? 'Cause I want to get started
31 right away!"
32      She was all groggy and said, "Get started on what?"
33      "On my book," I said. I told her about my idea and she
34 got really excited too. We stayed up the rest of the night
35 planning it out, making an outline, getting her publisher out

1 of bed. Well, on the phone I mean. Well, they're really good
2 friends and all, so Mom can do that sort of thing. So,
3 anyway, that's when we made the plan and that's when I
4 started to work, as a writer.
5 The book, we decided, would be divided into fifty-two
6 mini-chapters. Each chapter would be named after the state
7 that my mom was visiting at the time, but the chapter would
8 be about the family or people that I was staying with that
9 week. I wouldn't include their real names or anything, but
10 just little stories about funny things they did, or
11 idiosyncrasies they had.
12 That was the plan and that's what I've been doing for
13 fifty-one weeks. Yep, it's been almost a year. Mom is coming
14 home in a week. She's leaving her car in Washington State
15 and flying home. I'm going to stay with my last host family
16 this week. That's what I call them in the book. I'm glad it's
17 almost over. It's been fun and I've written a lot of funny
18 stories. I think the funniest chapter is Texas. That week I
19 stayed with the Browns. Mrs. Brown is hilarious. It's really
20 funny because she doesn't even know that she is. She drove
21 me to school every morning with curlers in her hair and sang
22 old Judy Garland songs the whole way. She was pretty good
23 on "Somewhere Over the Rainbow." Then, at night when the
24 family was eating dinner, she'd pop the *Wizard of Oz* in the
25 DVD player. They never said a word to each other through
26 the whole meal, just sat there watching Dorothy and Toto.
27 Yeah, I'm glad Mom is coming home. There is absolutely
28 no one in this world like my mom. I found that out this year
29 for sure. I have missed her so much! And I've missed our
30 house. Dorothy was right, you know. There's no place like
31 home. There's no place like home.

# 35. Unplugged

1    Grandma, did Mom and Dad tell you why they sent me
2  here? Well, yeah, to spend time with you, but there's another
3  reason too. There's this boy ... that I like. And they don't
4  like him. They sent me here to get me away from him. They
5  sent me here to separate us. To keep us apart so that by the
6  time I get back in the fall I'll supposedly not even remember
7  his name or something. Andy. His name is Andy. Yeah, he's
8  my age. I don't know why they don't like him. They're just
9  being mean. No, no, it's not that I don't want to spend time
10 with you. Grandma, I didn't say that. Of course I love
11 spending time with you. It's just that, you're out here in the
12 country, and you don't have a computer. They took my cell
13 phone away from me too. I probably couldn't get a signal out
14 here anyway.
     Am I bored? No, not really. Well, sort of. I mean, it's not
15 you. I love being with you and I love your house. I just miss
16 Andy. Grandma! That's an awful way of putting it. The hots
17 for him? *(Laughs.)* **I guess so.** *(Shyly and seriously)* **I love him.**
18 And now I won't be able to talk to him all summer and when
19 I get back I'll still love him, but I'm worried. Will he still love
20 me? Grandma, I just have to call him. I know, I know it's
21 long distance and you can't have a big phone bill. I could pay
22 you back next year. I'm going to start baby-sitting in the fall
23 for that little girl Ana who just moved in next door.
24 Grandma, please!
25     *(Sighs.)* It's not the phone bill, is it? They made you
26 promise, didn't they? Not to let me use the phone to call
27 him. I knew it. *(Sighs.)* No, don't worry, I'm not mad at you.

78

1   You're only doing what they asked you to. They're so mean!
2   They don't know how great he is. They don't even want to
3   know. No, they didn't. They never gave him a chance. No,
4   they didn't. I'm telling you the truth! Grandma, why would I
5   lie to you? How can you even say that? You know I never
6   have. And I never will. They did not even want to get to
7   know him.
8       Do you think? Yeah, maybe. Yeah, that's probably true.
9   They probably don't want to face the fact that I'm growing
10  up. Is that how you felt when Mom brought Dad home? You
11  cried? You didn't like him? Why? No good reason? See,
12  that's the same with my parents and Andy. They don't have
13  a good reason. They don't have any reason. Grandma,
14  please, please let me call him. I just want to say hello. I
15  know, I know, you don't break your promises. No, I know.
16  *(Pause)* You have a better solution? Like, what? A letter?
17  Like, you mean, snail mail? Snail mail. That's what we call
18  it 'cause it's so much slower than email. You know, email,
19  that you send on the computer. *(Thinks about it.)* A letter.
20  *(Suddenly excited)* Grandma! You are so amazing. You are so
21  smart! Why didn't I think of that? You have stationery, too?
22  Oh, thank you. Oh, that's so pretty. And it smells like
23  *perfume.* Oh, Grandma, you are the coolest grandmother
24  that ever lived.

# 36. I Just Called to Say I Loathe You

1     Look, I just came by to say Happy Birthday. That's it.
2 And that I wish I'd never met you. Oh really? Really? You
3 don't wish that you had never met me? Yeah, I believe that.
4 You've had a really good time haven't you? Why? Why did
5 you do it? Why did you make me fall in love with you, when
6 you knew it could never be?
7     It must have been very entertaining. Very.
8     Mad? How long do I plan to stay mad? Let's see ... How
9 about forever? Oh, but I don't mean mad as in angry, like
10 you do. I mean mad as in crazy. Crazy because I'm in love
11 with you and no amount of reason or logic can make it go
12 away. I don't sleep anymore. I can't even eat. Do you know
13 how many times a day I pick up my cell phone to text you?
14 You never get it because I never send it! But I do it a
15 thousand times a day.
16     You knew this would happen and you knew that you
17 never planned to leave Chiara. You knew that and yet you
18 played me like a fool. You played me like that stupid electric
19 guitar of yours. You made it so exciting. Forbidden love.
20 Couldn't let it out in the open. Had to let Chiara down gently.
21 When the time was right. What a lie. Yes it was! You never,
22 ever intended to break up with her. Admit it! At least do me
23 that one favor and admit it to me! You knew you would never
24 break up with her and you knew that I would never tell her.
25 You used my friendship with Chiara. You knew I would never
26 be the one to tell my best friend that I had fallen in love with
27 her boyfriend. That I tried with all my heart and soul to take
28 him away from her. I have to admit it; you are one very

1  clever guy. One very manipulative guy. You really made me
2  think that you had fallen in love with me. And now I know it
3  was all a big joke. You sank to such a low level and I
4  followed right behind you.
5      Yeah, thanks, I know. It was my choice and I made it and
6  I'm no better than you. You're right. You are soooo right.
7  But, you know what, there's something you just don't get.
8  I thought this was for real. I fell in *love.* Do you even know
9  what the word means? I thought that this was fate. That we
10  couldn't help ourselves, you know. Like Romeo and Juliet.
11  Star-crossed lovers.
12      So, I forgive myself, but I can't forgive you and I can't
13  forget. Why? Why can't I forgive you? Because you did it for
14  fun! You did it like, I don't know, for some kind of thrill.
15  Some sort of challenge. Or did you do it to hurt me? Yes.
16  That's it, isn't it? Well, you did hurt me. And you really
17  screwed up my life. But, anyway, why I'm going on and on
18  and why I came here, I have no idea. Oh, yeah, to say Happy
19  Birthday I guess.
20      Chiara called me all excited. She told me all about your
21  present and how her mother is loaning her the car so she
22  can take you to dinner. She has no clue. She thinks
23  everything's just great. She thinks I'm her best friend. I
24  wish I had been. A real friend to her, that is. Then maybe
25  I'd be sleeping at night. Maybe my life wouldn't be falling
26  apart. Happy Birthday. I'll always ... hate you.

# 37. A Deeper Depression

1    Mom, I'm worried about Dad. He's depressed. Don't tell
2    him that I told you. He'd be so mad. But he is. Well, yeah,
3    it's that and other things too. I mean, of course he's not
4    thrilled that you're getting remarried, but it's a lot of other
5    things. Things that I can't really tell you. I mean, he'd be
6    very upset if I did. Well, OK, I can tell you the gist of it I
7    guess. It's money too. And his job. And there's this woman
8    that he asked out at work who didn't want to go. (Sighs.)
9    Please, please don't tell him that I'm telling you all this. But
10   it's just that I don't have anyone else to talk to, and ... I'm
11   scared. I don't like seeing him like that. I mean, you
12   remember how he gets. Yeah, all down in the dumps,
13   doesn't want to do anything. Yeah, that sort of thing, only
14   it's a little worse sometimes lately.
15       Like yesterday. You called to say you'd be a few hours
16   late picking me up, so he says, "Hey, let's play some
17   chess." So I said "Sure," and we did. But as we got toward
18   the end, I was winning, I could see this like dark cloud come
19   over his face. He looks at his king and he looks at all the
20   pieces that I have left on the board and he gets all teary-
21   eyed. "This, Amanda, this," he says. "Let this be a lesson
22   to you for the future. You don't want to be the one left
23   standing alone. You need a support system, people who love
24   you and will be there for you. If you lose that, once that's
25   gone, it's checkmate."
26       Mom, what are we going to do? I mean, I've tried
27   everything. I tried to get him to play that game you used to
28   play with me, but nothing would work. You know, that game

1   where we would try to list all of our favorite memories in life.
2   You called it the "Moments of Happiness" game. We used to
3   laugh at how silly some of the moments were, but how when
4   we looked back they were some of our favorite memories.
5   Like the time it was raining and Buster fell asleep on my
6   stomach while I was reading a book. Remember? We
7   laughed because that moment was almost at the top of my
8   list. Well, that game just threw Dad into a deeper
9   depression. He said that all of his favorite memories made
10  him sad. *(Sighs.)* I wish there was something I could do.

# 38. Our First Kiss

1     *(RACHEL stands on the church steps, waiting. She looks at*
2     *her watch and sighs. Then she sees "him" at last. She speaks*
3     *rapidly.)*
4
5     Oh, Andrew! I'm so happy you came. You are so good to
6   me. Last night when you dropped me off at home, I thought
7   I might never see you again. But you came. You understood.
8   You know, a lot of guys would have been totally angry with
9   me for not letting them kiss me at the end of the date. But
10  it's like I told you, whenever I give a guy his first kiss it has
11  to be here on these church steps. You see, so many of the
12  monumental, momentous and sometimes outrageous
13  moments of my life have taken place here. Yes, monumental
14  and momentous.
15     Well, for instance, I used to have this tremendous crush
16  on Elliot Barker. And right here, on these church steps, is
17  the place where we were first introduced. Oh, don't worry,
18  that was long ago. That is ancient history now. But at the
19  time, Elliot, was the first thought on my mind in the morning
20  and the last thought before I lay my head down at night. I
21  used to dream of him and I getting married. Oh, I don't
22  mean at night in my sleep, but all day long. Daydream of
23  course. That's why I ended up getting a D in French last
24  year. Instead of listening to the conversational tapes, I
25  would sit and write Mrs. Rachel Barker over and over again.
26  Or, Mrs. Elliot Barker, in my very best penmanship. I would
27  even practice answering the phone in my bedroom. "Hello,
28  this is Mrs. Elliot Barker. Oh yes, I'll call my husband

1 straight away." Then I'd call, "Elliot. Elliot, dear." It sounds
2 quite silly, I know, but you see this is the extent to which
3 I'm capable of falling in love. And this, my dear Andrew, is
4 now exactly how I feel about you. And now that you've
5 agreed to meet here for our special occasion, I feel even
6 surer of my love for you. So Andrew dear, now our moment
7 has arrived. It's twilight. No one is around. The moment is
8 **just right.** *(She puckers up and closes her eyes and waits, but*
9 *nothing happens. She opens her eyes and looks around.)*
10 Andrew, my love? Where did you go?

# 39. Girl Painter

1    I may have been born in this neighborhood, but as far
2    back as I can remember, I just knew that I didn't belong
3    here. I think that's why I started painting. Kind of used it as
4    an escape. Well, not kind of, it was. It was my escape. I used
5    to dream of what it would be like to be a princess. I would
6    look at books in school that showed me there really were
7    princesses out there. Somewhere. I would lie in bed at night
8    and try to shut out the sounds from the street below by
9    imagining myself in an actual palace. I would look around
10    my room and imagine everything being coated in gold and
11    silver. My comb, my paintbrushes, and my easel.
12    My parents have always been supportive of my talent for
13    art. They would tell me, "*You* are not where you are from,
14    *you* are where you are headed to." But it still hurt when I'd
15    hear kids at school talk about my neighborhood and call it
16    "The Hood." And once I heard a reporter on TV call us "The
17    Slums." The slums. I hated that word and everything it
18    stood for. Mean people on the street. Broken glass
19    everywhere. I tried to paint myself out of that picture, but I
20    longed for the magical day when by some miracle I would be
21    whisked far away to enchanting lands to see all the things
22    I'd heard and read about. Like the Eiffel Tower for instance,
23    or the Danube River. I'd watch that movie *The Sound of*
24    *Music* and I'd picture myself running through the hills. Yeah,
25    it was definitely an obsession for me: a dream European
26    vacation. It was evident in every painting that I did. And, you
27    know, people say that visualization pays off and, in my case,
28    it sure did.

1     One day in art class my teacher, Mr. Dixon, announced
2    this contest for young artists. It was a chance in a lifetime
3    opportunity, he said. The prize? A dream trip for two to tour
4    Europe, all the museums, all the architectural landmarks,
5    and points of beauty. Every artist's dream. I went home that
6    night determined to win. I painted, and painted, and
7    painted, and painted ... You get the picture. I put that
8    contest before everything else in my life. And, of course, as
9    you've probably guessed by now, the miracle took place. I
10  won. Yes, I won. I think I'm still in shock, but Mr. Dixon, he
11  said that he wasn't surprised. He said I had the talent, but
12  more than that, I wanted it probably more than anyone else
13  in the world.
14     How was the trip? Oh, the trip was amazing. I took my
15  mom and we were just wined and dined as they say. We
16  went to London and saw Buckingham Palace. We went to
17  Paris and saw all the sights. Yes, the Eiffel Tower of course.
18  We ate like queens and were in the company of people
19  whose lives must be like a dream. I mean the jewelry that
20  some of the people wore and the clothes. The hotels we
21  stayed in were exquisite too. It was ... well, everything I'd
22  always dreamed of and more.
23     But of course it came to an end. And we got off the
24  plane and back into reality. We took the subway to "The
25  Hood." And there, nothing had changed. I saw the same old
26  homeless people in the streets and the same angry, mean
27  people too. I saw the broken glass and the litter and I tried
28  to hide it from my mother as I wiped away the tear that fell
29  from my eye. I helped her bring in our luggage and went
30  through the drab living room to my room. Waiting for me
31  just as I left it. Outside of the window I could hear the
32  sirens and the people yelling at each other. Everything was
33  still the same, except something inside of me had changed.
34  I wiped away more tears and went over to my easel, picked
35  up my paint brush, and began painting, not a castle, not the

1 Eiffel tower or objects covered in gold. I picked up my brush
2 and began painting the slums.

# 40. Her "Me Song"

1     Hey, Tara. I did it. I did what your sister Becca told me
2    to do. I wrote a letter to my mother. Don't you remember?
3    She said that I should write a letter to my mother telling her
4    all the things that really bother me about her. Then I could
5    just leave it on the breakfast table or read it to her some
6    night when I got up the courage. You don't remember that
7    big conversation we had at your house the other night? Wow.
8    Do you ever listen to anything I say? Are you listening now?
9    OK good. I want to read you the letter. No, I didn't give it to
10   my mother yet. I'm too scared. *(Sighs.)* Do you want to hear
11   it or not? OK. Here it goes.

12    "Dear Mom, I'm writing you this letter because I can't
13   talk to you anymore. You are either too busy or, if we are
14   talking, you are too busy with something that I've come to
15   call your 'Me Song.' You probably don't know what that
16   means, but if you'd record yourself one day in a
17   conversation and then listen to it a few times, maybe you'd
18   start to see what I mean. Mom, you only talk about yourself.
19   Your dates, your job, your clothes, your makeup, the guys
20   that flirt with you at the office. I thought that my teens
21   would be more about *me* dating and *me* telling *you* about
22   the guys I like at school, but it's not. Your 'Me Song' is
23   drowning me out.

24    The other day I was watching a show on TV where this
25   psychologist was telling everyone to get in touch with their
26   inner child, and you know what I thought? I thought about
27   you and how you are *way* too in touch with your inner child,
28   Mom. I am supposed to be the child. You need to get in

1   touch with your inner adult. I need a mother, not a

2   roommate. Is this making any sense?"

3       *(Sighs and looks at "Tara.")* **So, what do you think? Should**

4   **I give it to her? Yeah, I know. It's useless.** *(Puts the letter in*

5   *her pocket.)* **I'll never have the nerve to say it to her. It sure**

6   **was fun writing it though.**

# 41. An Actress's Nightmare

1     I had it again last night. The dream. My recurring dream.
2  Except it was longer than usual and more complex. I kept
3  thinking I wasn't dreaming. That it was real. In fact, I kept
4  telling everybody in the dream, "I dream this all the time
5  and now it's really happening." Weird, huh?

6     Well, yeah, it was just like it usually happens, the way I
7  usually dream it, but it was, like I said, longer. A lot longer.
8  And a lot more complex. Yeah, I was in the school play like
9  I usually am. I was in costume as usual. This time the
10  costume was this long flowing pink gown. It was kind of
11  Shakespearean looking, you know, sort of a Renaissance-
12  type gown, but as usual I didn't have the faintest idea what
13  the play was or who I was supposed to be.

14     So there I was, standing in the wings, in this beautiful
15  costume, in a total panic. I kept asking everyone, anyone
16  who walked by, if they had a script. And finally someone
17  gave me one. I asked the stage manager what page we were
18  on and at some point I was swept on to the stage with a
19  group of actors who seemed to be certain that I was
20  supposed to be with them. I followed along in the script until
21  everyone stopped talking and then I supposed it was my
22  turn and I read aloud.

23     Now, keep in mind this wasn't a rehearsal. The audience
24  was packed. The lights were on us and I was in a royal
25  sweat, but somehow I thought I was getting by. But then,
26  then … Mrs. Shirley came out onstage and everyone
27  stopped what they were doing. She looked right at me and
28  said, "Megan Little, why are you reading from a script? This
29  is a live show. Do you see the audience out there? Don't you

1 think they deserve a little more of a performance than that?"
2 Then she stomped off the stage and the scene continued.
3 But she had me so rattled that when it was my turn to speak
4 again, or should I say read, I could hardly do it. The words
5 were like sticky taffy in my mouth and I kept getting stuck.
6 Yeah, stuck.
7     Finally, I got stuck on "déjà vu." Yeah, déjà vu. I don't
8 know how I was saying it wrong, but I was definitely saying
9 it very wrong and I just couldn't seem to get past it. Finally,
10 this very loud lady in the first row shouts out, "It's déjà vu,
11 you idiot." Now that really made me mad, and I felt I had to
12 defend myself. I said, "For your information, I know déjà vu,
13 I totally know that word, ma'am. And, just so you know, the
14 only reason I'm reading my part tonight is because I haven't
15 been feeling well today. In fact, I've been very sick." Now, of
16 course that was a big lie, but I somehow felt it would help.
17     Anyway, the show kept going on and I found myself in
18 the wings once more looking out at the action on the stage.
19 For some reason I thought the curtain closed at one point
20 and I decided to cross the stage to the other side. Halfway
21 across I looked out and yep, you guessed it, the curtain was
22 not closed. I was walking across the stage in the middle of
23 a scene that I definitely didn't belong in. And so in the
24 middle of this dream I'm thinking, "Oh boy, I'll bet I'll hear
25 about this tomorrow."
26     Suddenly, the dream jumped to the next day and sure
27 enough I had heard about it and also heard I was being
28 kicked out of the show. And you know what? I felt so
29 relieved, 'cause I still didn't know what the name of the play
30 was or who I was. I walked out of the auditorium with all
31 eyes on me, people whispering, and shaking their heads. I
32 turned around and said, "Well, I had a nervous breakdown or
33 something. Oh well. Too much pressure, I guess." Weird
34 dream. Right?

# 42. What Bugs Me

1     OK. I see. Are you through? I mean, is that it? The end
2 of your list of things that bug you about me? It is? Oh good,
3 because believe it or not, and this may come as a big shock
4 to you, but there are just a few things about you that really
5 bug me. Yes, really. OK, to start with, you have this really
6 bad habit of saying offensive things to people in
7 conversation, but you always start off your offensive
8 statement by looking the person straight in the eye and
9 saying "No offense, but ... " Yeah, I've seen you do it a zillion
10 times. Like after Jenifer joined that new club at school, you
11 were like, "No offense, Jenifer, but I think that everyone in
12 that club is a complete dork." Or how about the night you
13 came over for dinner and my dad made us lasagna? You
14 were like, "No offense, Mr. Peterson, but my dad makes the
15 best lasagna in the world. I'll ask him to send you his recipe
16 sometime." Do you think that saying "No offense" before a
17 statement totally negates the offensiveness of your rude
18 remarks? Well, nobody else thinks so. And no, I don't
19 believe that you really meant no offense. And my dad was
20 crushed, by the way. We can't get him to cook anymore.
21 He's like, "I can't cook. Even my lasagna is second-rate."
22 You totally traumatized him.
23     OK, let's see, you know what else bothers me?
24 Something else you do that is kind of similar. In your
25 emails, you like to say this really mean or hurtful stuff and
26 then follow it with L-O-L or a little smiley face. What is that
27 all about? Am I supposed to think you're joking or just that
28 you think it's funny to be mean? L-O-L and Mr. Smiley Face

1    do not just give you the freedom to say whatever malicious
2    and derogatory comment you'd like. In fact, if I'm not
3    mistaken, L-O-L is supposed to be reserved for something
4    that is actually funny. And, if you think Merideth Baxter
5    falling on her face in gym class is hysterical, then I don't
6    think I really like you anymore. Merideth is a friend of mine.
7    Maybe I haven't known her for quite as long and we don't
8    know each other's little idiosyncrasies, but I think she's very
9    nice. And to quote someone who used to be my best friend:
10   no offense, but I think it would be much funnier if you fell on
11   your face in gym class, L-O-L. *(Puts a big insincere smile on*
12   *her face.)*

# 43. Nothing Ever Happens

1    I'm so bored. Absolutely nothing good ever happens
2 around here. Oh yeah? Like what? *(Waits.)* See, you can't
3 think of one stinkin' good thing that's happened in, like,
4 forever, right? *(Sighs.)* So, do you want to do anything?
5 Besides pick your nose. *(Laughs.)* You were too. I just saw
6 you. Oh come on, I'm only teasing. Oh come on, please
7 don't leave. I'll never say that again. Even if it's true.
8 *(Laughing)* I'm just kidding. Alright, come on, what do you
9 want to do? Want to play cards? Yeah, I know we did that
10 yesterday.

11    *(Thinking)* Hey, I've got it! Let's make prank calls. Oh
12 come on. It is not immature. OK, well maybe it is, but it's
13 fun. Geez Louise, what do you want to do then? I've come
14 up with two really good ideas and you've come up with
15 absolutely nothing. Zilch. Zero. Nada.

16    You do?! *(Hopeful)* You have a good idea? *(Disappointed)*
17 Paint our nails? Oh boy, that sounds thrilling. Oh really?
18 Since when is painting fingernails better than prank calling?
19 I mean, it's not like anybody's going to see our nails. It's not
20 like we have dates picking us up tonight to take us to the
21 Senior Prom or something. Yeah, the senior prom is tonight.
22 You're joking, right? You did not forget that it's tonight. You
23 are lying. Liar, liar, pants on fire, hanging off a telephone
24 wire. You have been thinking about this night for the last
25 three months. You have been fantasizing about Steven
26 Estevez asking you to the senior prom twenty-four hours a
27 day, seven days a week ever since you laid eyes on him. Oh
28 my gosh! You are so in denial. Yup. In denial. Look, you

1  should just admit that you're heartbroken and *(Imitating a*
2  *sophisticated psychologist)* let yourself feel the pain. Then, and
3  only then, can you start healing.
4      *(Ducking)* Hey, don't throw pillows. Come on! I mean it!
5  Seriously though, you should look at the situation with
6  Steven realistically. You are a freshman and he is a senior.
7  *(Thinks about it.)* A very hot senior. You have three more
8  years until your senior prom and by then some wonderful
9  guy is going to ask you to go and you will wear the most
10 beautiful dress in the world. And by then, maybe you'll even
11 have a chest. Hey! I said *stop with the pillows!* I know, I
12 know, of course you have a chest. Everyone has a chest. If
13 you didn't have a chest how could you possibly wear a shirt?
14 Hey, where are you going? You're bored? Of course you're
15 bored. So am I. It's like I said, absolutely nothing good ever
16 happens around here.
17     Don't go home! That will be even more boring. *(Suddenly*
18 *has a bright idea)* If you stay, I know what we can do. We can
19 make brownies. Yup. My mom bought a mix yesterday. Yup.
20 Want to? Awesome. Let's go girl, I'm starving. Who wants to
21 go to the stupid Prom when you can stuff your face with
22 chocolate brownies? Oh, do we have to? Oh, alright. After
23 the brownies we'll paint our nails.

# 44. The Angry Girl

1    Hey, what are you here for? Yeah, I know to see the
2  principal, but what did you do? Me? You're joking, right?
3  Wow, I guess you weren't here yesterday were you? You were
4  skipping? Oh man, you picked the wrong day to skip. Well,
5  yesterday is the reason I'm waiting to see Mr. Fogle this
6  morning. Hmph! My parents were supposed to come too,
7  but luckily they couldn't miss work.

8    Oh yeah, yesterday. Well, it all actually started last
9  week. I got fed up with *Mr. Fozak* and all his *stupid* sayings
10  so I told him so. Well no, not really to his face, but sort of.
11  I did it in writing. He gave us this *stupid* assignment to do
12  a "Top Ten" list of things. It was supposed to be like the top
13  ten reasons to do your homework, or not to take drugs, or
14  not to curse out your parents. You know, like a public
15  service announcement sort of thing. He said it was a contest
16  and that the winner was going to, like, say their list on the
17  morning announcements and, like, change people's lives or
18  something.

19    So, OK, well, you know how Mr. Fozak and I never get
20  along, right? Yeah, he's always calling me "the angry girl"
21  and stupid stuff like that. Well, you know, I never even try in
22  his class 'cause of that. I figure, why bother? He doesn't
23  think much of me, so why disappoint him, right? But when
24  he gave us that assignment I got this brilliant idea. I decided
25  to write the best possible list and win the contest. Then,
26  when I got to go to the office to read the list, I'd recite
27  another list that I'd written and I had memorized word for
28  word in my head: The top ten most annoying things that Mr.

1 Fozak says and does. Yeah, it was a pretty cool idea. Did it
2 work? Sure it worked. I mean it would have. I turned in this
3 great list called "The top ten reasons to never give up." It
4 was really sincere and moving and all that.
5     When Mr. Fozak announced that I had won the contest,
6 I swear I saw a tear in his eye. So, I won. I went to the office
7 yesterday morning ready to recite the *other* list, but when I
8 stepped up to the microphone I just couldn't do it. I looked
9 at the list in my hand, the winning list, and I got this really
10 strong feeling that some kid in a classroom out there really
11 needed to hear my list that day. And suddenly that just
12 seemed so much more important than telling Mr. Fozak
13 what I really thought of him. I read the list that I had written,
14 "The top ten reasons to never give up," and everyone in the
15 office, like, stopped what they were doing and listened. And
16 when I was done, they applauded and some of them even
17 stood up. Yeah, that's right. I got a standing ovation, I
18 guess. It felt really good. *(Pauses, lost in the memory.)* What's
19 that? Oh, so why am I here? Oh, the principal wants to give
20 me some sort of award or something. *(Rolls her eyes and
21 says, almost convincingly.)* How lame, right? I wonder what it
22 is.

# 45. Gone Fishin'

1   *(Sitting on a dock, holding a fishing rod. To her fishing*
2   *buddy)* **Wow!** *(Wiping forehead)* **We've been out here for an**
3   **hour now and nothing!** *(Sighs.)* **Do you really think this is**
4   **fun? You do. Me? Oh yeah,** *(Rather sarcastic)* **I'm having a**
5   **great time. I haven't had this much fun since I had three**
6   **teeth pulled out all at once, without Novocaine. No, I'm just**
7   **kidding. This is really not bad. I mean, sitting in the sun, for**
8   **an hour, doing absolutely nothing, catching absolutely**
9   **nothing. This is great.**
10      **Hey! What's that? Do you have something? Oh my gosh!**
11  **It's a ... shoe!** *(Laughing)* **You caught a shoe.** *(Seeing that her*
12  *buddy isn't finding this funny)* **I mean, darn, that's terrible. A**
13  **shoe is just soooo disappointing. Gosh. It's just soooo ...**
14  *(Smothering a laugh)* **depressing. Don't worry, the next one**
15  **will be a fish, a real big fish. I mean, a ... whale, or**
16  **something like that.**
17      *(Looks out at the water, then at her buddy.)* **This is really**
18  **important to you, isn't it? I mean, fishing and all that. Hey,**
19  **are you crying? Oh, OK. No, of course not. Yeah, well it's**
20  **really hot out here. I'm sweating too.**
21      *(Looking down at the water, starts whistling)* **You know, I'm**
22  **sorry I was ... making fun of this earlier. I mean fishing. You**
23  **know, I can see how you could kind of get to know**
24  **somebody better this way. You know, spending time, just**
25  **waiting for a fish. Oh, I mean, of course that's not why you**
26  **do it. I mean, it's totally about catching a fish. Yeah, a huge**
27  **gigantic fish of some sort. And then you clean it, right? And**
28  **bone it. And then you fry it up in a big shiny pan. That's**

1   what it's all about, but ... if in the meantime, I mean all the
2   while you're waiting for some big fish to just come along and
3   bite, you just might get to know your fishing buddy a little
4   better. Like, while we're sitting here, we could just shoot the
5   breeze and while we're shooting the breeze, we might just
6   find out ... stuff. You know? Stuff that we would have
7   otherwise never told each other. Right?
8        No? It's just about the fish? OK. Well, while I'm waiting
9   for my fish, I'm gonna tell you something that I've never told
10  you before. If that's OK. OK, here it goes. You know, when
11  I first came to this town, I didn't know a single soul and I
12  felt so down. So ... low. And I felt like I had no friends. No,
13  that's true. I didn't just feel like I had no friends, I really,
14  truly, didn't have any friends. No, no, I really didn't. But
15  then, I met you. You were so ... nice to me. So kind. And it
16  really meant a lot to me. I never told you before, but I wanted
17  to, and now ... I did. So, I'm glad, you know, that we came
18  out here today so that I could tell you that. Even if it doesn't
19  mean anything to you. Even if this is all about the fish. Hey!
20  Oh my gosh! Hey! Help! What do I do? I have a bite!

# 46. Blowout

1     *(Sitting by herself in front of a birthday cake. Singing.)*
2 **Happy Birthday dear Lani. Happy Birthday to me.** *(Takes a*
3 *deep breath and blows out the candles, but they don't all go out*
4 *until the third try.)* **Three years. I'll have to wait three years**
5 **to marry Harrison Fineberg.** *(Sighs.)* **Oh well. That's good in**
6 **a way. That gives me more time.**
7     *(To the audience)* **You see, Harrison Fineberg doesn't even**
8 **know I exist. No, seriously. I mean, I know some people say**
9 **that sort of thing about other people when they think**
10 **they're, like, unimportant to them or something, but this is**
11 **for real, Harrison Fineberg doesn't know I exist. But I on the**
12 **other hand, I not only am aware of his existence, but I am**
13 **madly in love with him. I know, you're probably wondering**
14 **how that could be possible. Well, it is. It is possible.**
15     **You see, well, it's kind of an interesting story really. I**
16 **mean, I met Harrison at a Halloween party two years ago. I**
17 **had gone to the party to spy on my boyfriend. Well, my ex-**
18 **boyfriend. We had broken up, but I couldn't get over him.**
19 **So, I found out that he was invited to this party and I went.**
20 **But I went in a disguise. I mean, nobody could tell who I**
21 **was. Not even my best friend Sheila. Well, I told everyone**
22 **my name was Madame La Rue and I used this different**
23 **voice.** *(Laughing at the memory)* **It was sort of like this**
24 **"Helloooo, my name, da'ling, is Madame La Roooo." It was**
25 **quite hilarious. And even though my ex never did show up,**
26 **Harrison was there. And I knew from the first moment that**
27 **I saw him. He was with some preppy girl named Lisbeth.**
28 **She was all dressed up in this French maid costume, but**

1   when I was doing my Madame La Rue act, Harrison found it
2   especially funny. Yeah, that's right. Harrison fell in love with
3   Madame La Rue, and she ... I, fell in love with him.
4       But then, the party ended and before I knew what was
5   happening, Harrison and his little Lisbeth were gone. But I
6   was in love. And I did a little research on the Internet and
7   found out all about Harrison. What school he went to, where
8   he lived. And I've done nothing but plan our life together
9   ever since. After we finish college of course. He's going to
10  Notre Dame. Well, you probably think this is crazy, but you
11  know what? I know that he and I are meant to be. And if I
12  have to wait three years, that's OK. *(Singing again)* **Happy**
13  **Birthday to me.**

# 47. What a Difference a Day Makes

1     Huh? Oh, I'm sorry, I don't mean to be ignoring you. I'm
2  just ... sort of lost ... in thought. *(Sighs.)* I'm ... I mean, my
3  mind is on something. Sorry. What were you saying? No,
4  please, really, go ahead. *(Sighs.)* So, now you're not going to
5  talk. *(Sighs and rolls her eyes.)* You know, if you knew what
6  was on my mind, what's distracting me, you wouldn't have
7  the heart to be so vindictive. Yes, you are. You're being
8  vindictive. Not even a little? *(Sighs.)* Oh well. It's OK. I don't
9  care. I don't think I care about anything anymore. What's
10 wrong? Oh, just about everything. But I don't think I can
11 talk about it just yet. But I want to. I need to tell someone.
12 I just feel so stupid. *So* stupid, because I never had a clue.
13    OK, OK. I know, I mean I'm sure that I'm making you
14 curious, but I just ... I can't talk about this like it's
15 happening to me. It's too surreal. I mean, it just doesn't
16 seem real and yet, if I tell you what's on my mind, I think ...
17 I won't be able to get through it without getting hysterical.
18 And this is not where I want to get hysterical: study hall.
19 *(With exasperation)* What am I going to do? I know, I know,
20 how can you help me if I don't tell you. But how can I tell
21 you when I can't talk about it? Huh? What do mean? Oh, like
22 they always do in the movies: "I have this friend who stole
23 a car or is pregnant, or whatever." And all the while
24 everybody knows that they're talking about themselves. No!
25 Of course I didn't steal a car. And I am definitely not
26 pregnant. Are you crazy?
27    OK, OK, well I'll try to tell you. I'll try to act it out like
28 we're in the movies. I mean, I have this friend, OK? She's

1   really upset because she ... found something out yesterday
2   that is sort of ... life-altering. I mean, she should have been
3   able to figure it out for herself years ago. All the clues were
4   there. I mean, she's not an idiot or anything, but she really
5   feels like one. OK, OK, I'm getting to the point. Hold your
6   horses.
7       *(Takes a deep breath.)* **You see, yesterday, she was this**
8   **happy teenager with a great family: mother, father, and**
9   **brother. And then, last night her mother and father came**
10  **into her bedroom and looked all weird like they'd been**
11  **crying. Then, they sat down on the edge of her bed and told**
12  **her that she was ... not really their child. That she was**
13  **adopted.** *(Looking straight ahead)* **They didn't want to ever**
14  **have to tell her, but, as it turns out, her birth mother has**
15  **found her and has been trying to make contact. And they**
16  **wanted her to hear it from them first.** *(Closes her eyes, then*
17  *looks down for a moment. Finally to her friend)* **So, you see, this**
18  **friend of mine is pretty devastated. It's like I feel like, I mean**
19  *she* **feels like, she sort of died last night, or she was just**
20  **born. It changes everything.**

# 48. Schadenfreude

1　　Schadenfreude. It's a German word. What does it mean?
2　It means when you hear that someone else is experiencing
3　problems, bad times, or misfortunes, you experience
4　enjoyment, pleasure, etcetera, etcetera, etcetera. Sound
5　familiar? Sound like a word that you can relate to, Jose?
6　What am I talking about? I'm talking about you and the way
7　you are and how last week when I was reading this article,
8　this review of a movie I wanted to see, the article talked
9　about a character in the movie and the word that they used
10　was "Schadenfreude." So, I looked it up and you know
11　what? After I read the definition, I was almost surprised that
12　they didn't have your picture in there. And you know what,
13　I'm not the only one who thinks this word somehow relates
14　to you.
15　　I went to talk to Mrs. English, you know, my English
16　teacher this year. Yeah, yeah, I know, no pun intended, of
17　course. (Sarcastically) Yeah, how hilarious. Anyway, I went to
18　talk to Mrs. English about this word and I was like, "Hey
19　Mrs. English, I found this totally, most amazing word last
20　night, and I was wondering if you could include it in our
21　vocabulary lesson this week?" So, she was like so excited
22　that I had made the suggestion and she totally agreed to do
23　it. So, she did, and you know what? Well, I'll tell you what.
24　On our vocabulary quiz she asked us to use every word in a
25　sentence. And you know what else? She let me grade the
26　papers. And you know what else? Everybody's sentence had
27　your name in it. Um, let's see if I can remember some of
28　them. Oh, yeah, here's one, "Jose Mendez is a good

1 example of Schadenfreude." Or how about "Last week,
2 when I fell down the stairs, I could tell by Jose's behavior
3 that he was experiencing Schadenfreude." And I could go on
4 and on. A mere coincidence, Jose? Or is there a message in
5 all this? You know, I was in utter disbelief when I was
6 grading those papers.
7     But I definitely felt validated in my opinion that you are
8 the personification of Schadenfreude. In fact, I'm so sure
9 that you are that I am going to do you the great favor of
10 making your day. How? Well, I'll tell you. Although the
11 majority of the class used the word Schadenfreude in a
12 sentence correctly, they unfortunately hadn't bothered to
13 study any of the other words. So, eighty percent of the class
14 failed. See! I knew that would put a smile on your face.

# 49. The Doctor Is In?

1    Dr. Petrias, thank you so much for agreeing to see me
2  on such short notice. I know that new patients usually have
3  to wait months, but I'm not sure if I could wait that long.
4  Well, thank you. Um, yes, now I need to tell you why I'm
5  here. Well, it's like I told the nurse on the phone, I've had
6  this problem for a while. Well, it's not really a problem, at
7  least I haven't felt that it was, but it's kind of gotten out of
8  hand. Well, yes, I know. I do have to tell you what the
9  problem is if you're going to help me, don't I?
10    Well, Dr. Petrias, do you think it's normal to have an
11  imaginary friend? Uh-huh. Yeah. Uh-huh. That's what I
12  thought you'd say. I mean, that's what I'd read. I mean, that
13  it's normal for little kids, but kind of abnormal if it continues
14  past a certain age. Well, you see, that's my problem, Dr.
15  Petrias. *(Sighs.)* I have an imaginary friend who has been
16  with me since, oh, around first grade. What's that? Oh, you
17  want me to tell you about my imaginary friend. Well, um, I
18  guess I first started talking to her, um, like I said around
19  first grade, because we lived in a really lonely, sort of
20  deserted neighborhood, and I didn't have any other kids to
21  play with. When I wasn't at school that is. So, I made up
22  this friend named Lisa. She and I used to spend hours
23  together playing school. What's she like? Oh, she's really
24  funny, but sometimes aggravating. Just like a real person, I
25  guess.
26    So, *(Sighs)* anyway, the problem is Dr. Petrias, she's
27  never really gone away, you know. I mean, I still talk to Lisa.
28  I mean, now we don't play school or anything, but I ... well,

1    I take her shopping. We go to movies. And she loves fast
2    food, so I'm always taking her through the drive-thru. And
3    she doesn't have her license yet, so I'm always the one that
4    drives. What's that? Oh, yeah, of course I realize that she's
5    not real, but I've spent so much time with her that, well, it
6    almost seems like she is. Uh-huh. Oh I see. So, I'll come
7    back once a week for a while and work on this situation, I
8    mean with this imaginary friend. Uh-huh. That sounds good.
9    OK.
10      Oh, but, Dr. Petrias, I haven't really told you the whole
11   story yet. Well, you see, around ninth grade Lisa started
12   dating somebody named Jim. Yeah, I mean, my parents
13   won't let me date boys until I go to college, but Lisa just
14   strolled right into our house with him one day. Oh, well,
15   yeah, I mean, Jim's imaginary too, and yes, of course I made
16   him up. I know that. But, it's like, Lisa really loves him and
17   I just couldn't take him away from her after I saw how crazy
18   she was about him and all that. Oh, OK, so then I'll start
19   coming to therapy twice a week? Oh, OK. Wow, this is so
20   great, Dr. Petrias. I really, really appreciate it. I mean, with
21   your busy schedule and all that. You know Lisa was right
22   about you. I mean, I know you can't talk about other
23   patients and all that, but Lisa confided in me the other day
24   that she's been coming here for years and she thinks the
25   world of you.

# 50. Interrupted

1     *(Dancing wildly and suddenly stops)* **Hey! Who turned off**
2 **the music?** *(Spins around and sees who it was.)* **Mom? Dad?**
3 **What ... what are you doing here?** I mean, I thought you
4 weren't coming back until Thursday. Oh. OK. Well, um, gee,
5 welcome home. We're just ... I mean, I just, um, invited a
6 few friends over for a little celebration. **Um. What are we**
7 **celebrating?** Oh, um, I think um, oh yeah, uh, Caroline and
8 I both got As on our biology project. Yeah, right Caroline?
9 Oh, um, Caroline you haven't met my parents yet, have you?
10     **What's that, Mom?** Oh, yeah, I guess, you probably
11 haven't met most of these people, right? Pardon me, Dad?
12 Oh, well, that's not a terrible idea, I guess. Yeah, maybe as
13 everyone goes out the door I should introduce them to you.
14 Yeah, um, I mean, yes sir, that's not a bad idea. OK. *(Sighs.)*
15 OK, folks. I'm sorry, but the party is over. Um, my parents,
16 I mean, I didn't ask my parents if I could do this and well,
17 they're home now, as you can see, and they aren't OK with
18 it. So, if, well, I guess if you don't mind, please, everybody,
19 let's call it a night and I'll see you soon.
20     *(Sighs.)* **This is really embarrassing, and I'm really sorry.**
21 **What's that, Mom?** Oh, yeah, um, guys, listen, please pick
22 up any trash that might be on the floor or anywhere else on
23 your way out. *(Starts picking up stuff.)* **Geez, I didn't realize we**
24 were being this messy. I'm sorry, Mom. I'm sorry, Dad. But,
25 I mean, we were just having fun. Oh well, I can't seem to do
26 anything right, can I? Huh? Oh, bye Carla. Yeah, OK, talk to
27 you tomorrow. Bye John. Bye, everyone. Huh? Oh yeah, go
28 ahead and take whatever you brought. Kara, don't forget to

1   get your brownies out of the kitchen. OK, well, bye.
2   *(Shuts the door.)* **Well, that's it. Everybody's gone. What?**
3   *(Turns around.)* **Oh geez. Um, what were you guys doing**
4   **upstairs?** *(Turns to her parents.)* **I told everyone to stay down**
5   **here, I swear.** *(To her friends on the stairs)* **Everyone's gone**
6   **because my parents are home and you guys need to leave**
7   **too. Thanks for listening, by the way. Didn't you hear me tell**
8   **everyone that upstairs was off limits?** *(Looks at her parents.)*
9   **I'm going to be grounded for life, aren't I? OK, great. Just**
10 until I turn twenty-one. Well, so much for my life. Bye guys,
11 hope you had fun.

# Monologues
# for Guys

# 1. The Problem is ...

1      Stop right there. Did you hear that? Say what you just
2 said again. No, no, you were saying, "The problem is ... "
3 and that right there, brother, is the problem. Your problem.
4      I think in this whole week at camp you've started a
5 sentence with that phrase about, well, at least about fifty
6 times. What are you, some kind of problem tracker? What
7 am I talking about? I'm talking about you, man, and your
8 attitude. Your outlook on life. Dude. You're young, you're not
9 too terrible at sports, you're kind of smart, and some of the
10 girls are even stupid enough to think you're "cute." At least
11 that's what I've heard them say.
12      But man, you are always so *down*. "The problem is,
13 there isn't anything to do at this camp." Or, "The problem
14 is, I'd rather be spending the summer with my cousin in
15 Hawaii." Hey, we'd all like to be spending the summer in
16 Hawaii, but you're starting to sound like a whiner. What am
17 I saying? I'm saying that you are a whiner! That's it! That's
18 the problem. *The problem is,* I got stuck at camp with a
19 first-rate, number-one whiner. I can't call you that? Why
20 not? It's a free country, and hey, if the shoe fits you got to
21 wear it, bro. Whiner. Whiner. Whinerrrrr.
22      *(His roommate, "Peter," runs out the door.)* **That's right, run**
23 **out the door. Go and tell the camp counselor.** *(Shouting after*
24 *him)* **You've been whining so much this past week he**
25 **probably won't even listen to you anymore. I bet that there**
26 **isn't one single person in camp that wants to listen to you**
27 **anymore.** *(Sighs and sits on the edge of the bed shaking his*
28 *head.)* **What a whiner. Probably gonna go and call home to**

113

1 Momma. Probably ask to get me kicked out of his room.
2 *(There's a knock at the door. He gets up and answers it.)* **Oh,**
3 **hi girls. Come on in. Peter?** Oh, well, um, yeah, he just left.
4 He had something that he suddenly remembered he had to
5 do. But I'm sure he'll be back. Want some chips and soda?
6 Yeah, we've got a stash. Well, Peter does. His mom sends
7 him tons of stuff, but *(Laughs and thinks about it for a minute)*
8 the problem is, I usually am the one that eats it all. Oh, but
9 he doesn't mind. We're really good friends. Yeah, great
10 friends. Peter? Yeah, he's a really great guy. Yeah, have a
11 seat. Go ahead. He's got some chocolate over here too. His
12 aunt who lives in Hawaii sent it to him. Yeah, it's awesome.
13 Do you like macadamia nuts? Me too. Yeah, I guess I am
14 lucky to have Peter for a roommate. *(Looks at the door.)* **Um,**
15 don't go anywhere girls, but I just remembered there's
16 something I got to do. *(Runs out the door calling)* **Peter! Dude!**
17 **Come back!**

# 2. Bagging It

1    (Bagging groceries at the end of a very busy checkout line)
2    Hello, ma'am. Would you like paper or plastic? OK. (Starts
3    putting the groceries in a paper bag.) Wow, these look really
4    good. Are they? Oh, you haven't tried them yet? Oh, well,
5    I'll bet they're really good. (Sticks a few more things in the
6    bag.) Boy, oh, boy, I love these too! Oh, wow, it must be
7    getting close to lunchtime. I sure am hungry. Well, ma'am,
8    would you like me to help you take your bags to the car?
9    No? Alrighty then. Have a good day.
10    Hello there, sir. How are you today? Would you like paper
11    or plastic? OK. (Starts putting everything in a plastic bag.)
12    Ooooh. Gross. What is this? Tongue? Oh my ... (Covers his
13    mouth like he's going to gag.) You eat this? (Puts it in the bag,
14    then smiles.) Oh well. (Shaking his head) To each his own.
15    Would you like some help taking this out to your car, sir?
16    Oh, yeah, that's true. It's just one bag. But there's a tongue
17    in it. (Sticks his tongue out and makes horror movie sounds.
18    Laughing) Have a good day, sir.
19    (Looks at his watch and says to the cashier) Hey Millie, it's
20    only nine thirty-five. The time is sure passing by slow this
21    morning. I can't even take a break until ten. Oh, good
22    morning Miss, would you like paper or plastic? Neither? Oh,
23    you brought your own bag. Awesome! One of those
24    environmental freaks I see. Oh, I mean, I don't mean freak
25    in a bad way.
26    (Putting some groceries in the bag) Freak to me just
27    means, um ... Millie, what's the word I'm looking for? Oh
28    yes, thank you Miss, activist. You're an environmental

1 activist. Well, pretty much everybody is gonna have to be an
2 environmental activist soon because we're gonna start
3 selling those bags and we're not gonna let our customers
4 pick plastic or paper anymore. Isn't that right, Millie? See,
5 my dad's a manager at the store on Fifty-Third Street, so I
6 get in on all the news before everyone else here. By the way,
7 if you are ever looking for a job, I'm the guy that can hook
8 you up. Just one word from me to my dad and you'll be
9 checking groceries, like Millie here, in a heartbeat. Oh, OK.
10 Well, would you like some help with this out to your car? Oh,
11 OK. Well, have a good day, Miss. Don't forget to recycle and
12 all that. That's really important you know. Preserves the
13 plastic trees.
14     *(Shaking his head and laughing)* **Plastic trees.** *(To "Millie")*
15 Hey, that was a pretty good one, huh Millie? You didn't hear
16 me? Well, she was leaving and I said, "Don't forget to recycle
17 and ... " Oh, I'm sorry. Hello, ma'am. Would you like paper
18 or plastic?

# 3. I Saw Everything

1     Hello, Mr. Anderson. Mrs. Simpson told me you wanted
2  to see me, and I came right away. Well, I mean, of course I
3  came right away, right? I mean, when the principal wants to
4  see you, you go right away, but what I mean is I was hoping
5  that you would want to see me because of the graffiti in the
6  hall in building three. That is why you wanted to see me?
7  Awesome! Well, I mean, that's really good, because I wanted
8  to see you about that same exact thing. I mean, you
9  probably think I did it, right? Well, Mr. Anderson, I'm here
10 to tell you, cross my heart and hope to die, that I did not, I
11 repeat, did not do it.

12     But, I have some really good news. Mr. Anderson, you
13 are in luck, because I saw the whole thing. Yep. That's right.
14 And I can tell you who the culprit is. Well, that is, the culprit
15 and her accomplice. Mr. Anderson, it's a good thing that
16 you're sitting down, because if you were standing, before I
17 laid this on you, I'd have to say, "Mr. Anderson, you'd better
18 have a seat." You know, like they do in the movies. The
19 detective comes into some guy's apartment to tell him the
20 bad news, like maybe the thief that stole all of his money
21 was his mother or somebody like that. OK. I'm sorry. You're
22 right, Mr. Anderson, I should really get to the point. Man,
23 you're good at this, Mr. Anderson. But then that's why they
24 give you the big bucks, eh?

25     OK. Sorry, sir. Yes, the point. The point is that I saw
26 who did it. I was right there and I saw them do it. Well, I
27 shouldn't say "do it" 'cause I really just saw them finish it
28 up. I mean, if I'd been there when they'd started it I would

1 have said something. I mean, I would have made them stop.
2 Or, you know, if they wouldn't have listened, I would have at
3 least told them to use better colors. You know. And by the
4 way, Mr. Anderson, if you don't believe me when I tell you
5 who did it, that's my other proof that I didn't do it. I am a
6 much better artist than that. You can ask Mr. Price.
7     OK, OK. I'll tell you. But Mr. Anderson, it's gonna be
8 hard. I mean, I hope you're not the kind of guy who does
9 impulsive things like ask for a divorce before he gets
10 couple's therapy or anything. Why am I mentioning a
11 divorce? Well, Mr. Anderson, in case you haven't guessed by
12 now, the graffiti artist was ... well, the artist was your wife,
13 Mrs. Anderson. Mr. Anderson, don't laugh. It's true. And
14 the accomplice, Mr. Anderson, was that old librarian, Mrs.
15 Carter.

# 4. Funny People

1     "What's it like having parents who are funny?" That's
2 what everyone wants to know. That's usually one of the first
3 questions I get when people meet me. And I'm always like,
4 "Beats the heck out of me." Seriously. I have no idea. My
5 parents, in our house, in our lives, our *real* lives, are *not*
6 funny. In fact, they are anything but funny.

7     Now, if someone were to ask me the question, "What's
8 it like having parents who are *famous* for being funny," then
9 I'd know what to say. It sucks. Well, for me it sucks. Maybe
10 for some other terrific, funny guy it would be great. But when
11 your parents are famous for being funny, somehow everyone
12 expects you to be. And when you're not, they're like, "What
13 happened to you? You're not funny *at all*." And you want to
14 say, "Hey, my parents aren't really funny either. Not in real
15 life. They just act like they're funny and happy and that's
16 what they do for a living. But at home, they're totally morbid
17 cynics." They are. That is, when they talk. They don't talk
18 much 'cause they're usually "exhausted" from doing "the
19 tour." They're always mad at someone too. Like usually
20 their manager, or some stupid critic, or maybe they're just
21 busy hating everybody, especially the "idiots" that pay to
22 see them. "The morons" that they have to talk down to in
23 order to get a laugh.

24     So you see? Are you getting the picture? What's really
25 weird is that I've had all this trouble with depression. I
26 mean, not just a *little* trouble, like "man, I'm so depressed,
27 I can't get a date," or some stuff like that. No, my problems
28 have been ... typically pretty major. Like, I needed to be,

1 you know, hospitalized a couple times. "Committed." Once,
2 it was like, almost to the point of no return. You know what
3 I mean? And my parents, man, they really have gone to
4 great lengths to make sure the media doesn't catch wind of
5 it. That might cast a shadow on their fun-loving, laugh-a-
6 minute images, you know? And we wouldn't want that,
7 would we? Hey, but I don't mean to sound sarcastic or
8 ungrateful or anything. God knows I wouldn't want the
9 media to find out either. That's not what I want to be
10 famous for. Being "crazy." Nah.
11     Actually, I don't really want to be famous for anything. I
12 mean, I've seen what it's done to my parents. Money? The
13 money is great. Obviously. I mean, who doesn't want
14 money. But maybe it's better when you can sell something
15 other than yourself in order to get it, right? Geez, my
16 parents, they're like products. Commodities. They're, like,
17 something that people buy. And if they don't measure up to
18 their customers' expectations, their beloved audience will,
19 you know, disappear, or heckle them, or want their money
20 back. My parents always say, "In the stand-up business,
21 you're only as good as your last punch line."
22     *(Sighs.)* You're probably getting sick of hearing about all
23 this, right? I mean, you asked me a question expecting to
24 hear about how great it is being me and how my parents
25 keep me in stitches twenty-four hours a day and all that.
26 Right? Sorry to be so disappointing. No, I am. I know I am.
27 It's OK. I'm used to it. Once, when I was "committed" for a
28 few days, you know, just so they could "keep an eye on
29 me," I overheard these two nurses talking. This one nurse is
30 like "Wow, I couldn't believe it when I found out who his
31 parents are." And the other one says, "Yeah, how did they
32 end up with *this* kid? They're such *funny people.*"

# 5. Understandin' Mama

1    My dad always says, "Your mama is a real piece of
2  work." You're probably thinkin', "Well, dads are always
3  sayin' somethin' like that." But in my case, it is darn right
4  true. My mama is a real piece of work. Yup. I figured that
5  out when I was jus' a kid. I didn't figure her out exactly, but
6  I figured out that she was … well, a "force to be reckoned
7  with" as they say. And I knew that if I was smart, well, I'd
8  watch my back. See, my mama is like one of them
9  kangaroos that tucks things in their pouch and you don't
10  know what she's got in there. Only with Mama, it ain't
11  gonna be some cute little hoppin' roo that's gonna pop out.
12  Nah, it's gonna be a much bigger surprise than that. See,
13  Mama likes to tuck away little grudges and things that you
14  said and done that you'd like to forget, but she never will.
15  Oh lord no, she never, ever will forget anythin'. And don't let
16  her fool you that she has. 'Cause Mama, that there is an A-
17  number-one actress. I mean, you could put her up against
18  the biggest movie star in the world and she'd win the award.
19    I'll tell ya. See, like I said, she likes to tuck away little
20  things that ya done that she didn't like, or things that ya
21  said in the heat of an argument or when ya was feeling all
22  cocky for one reason or another, like ya was too big for ya
23  britches or somethin'. Then she stews on it and she starts
24  plannin' and schemin' and pretendin' all the while that she
25  done forgot about the whole incident. But she's a plannin'
26  alright and that there woman is gonna get ya in the end.
27  And it's gonna be when ya least expect it. Yeah, Mama is a
28  real piece of work alright.

1    Well, I still remember when I got my first taste of jus'
2    what a piece of work she was. I was knee high to a
3    grasshopper. I was. Well, just about four years old. And part
4    of this story I'm tellin' is from my memory and part of this
5    story is what I remember from the retellin' I used to hear
6    done by old Granny Nell. Yeah, Granny Nell and a few others
7    like to tell this story. It's kind of a classic in these parts ya
8    might say.
9        So anyway. I was about four-years-old and as Granny
10   Nell tells it, I had takin' to tellin' a fib or two here and there.
11   Well, as Mama tells it, it was more like I was headin' on the
12   path to bein' a darn right pathological liar. Yup. Must-a been
13   real bad. But I can't for the life of me remember what the
14   heck I was lyin' about. I actually got up the nerve to ask my
15   mama about it one day a couple years back. I said, "Mama,
16   what does a four-year-old lie about anyway?" She gave me
17   this look, with her one good eye, and she says, "Some of
18   them will lie to ya about just about everythin'." Then she
19   shakes her head and says to me, "Boy, you just better
20   count yer blessin's that I saved ya from bein' the
21   pathological liar ya was on the path to becomin'." Then she
22   slammed down her skillet and stomped out of the room.
23       So, I still don't rightly know what I was lyin' about. But
24   I sure do remember what Mama did about it. Yup. It was a
25   hot summer day and we was ridin' back in the truck after
26   goin' into town. All of a sudden Mama says, "Son, ya sure
27   have been wantin' a pony for some time now, haven't ya?" I
28   guess I said, "Yes, Mama," or some fool thing like that. And
29   she says, "Well, son, when we get home you get yourself into
30   the barn and yer gonna find the cutest little cream colored
31   pony you ever did see and she is all yers." Well, ya can
32   imagine how happy I was. I was beside myself. I was
33   jumping up and down on that seat like I had ants in my
34   pants. Yes, sir. I sure do remember bein' excited about that
35   little pony.

1    Mama said, "What are ya gonna call it, son?" I said, "Is
2    it a girl or a boy?" And she said, "She's a girl. A real sweet
3    little girl pony." And I knew right then that I was gonna call
4    her Riley, 'cause that was the name of a beautiful little pony
5    that I had fallin' in love with at the fair that summer. So
6    Mama said, "Oh, yer gonna have many a fine hour with that
7    pony Riley. She's gonna be like yer new best friend." Well, I
8    was laughin' with excitement. When we got to the house I
9    sprung open the door and ran into the barn. When I got
10  inside I looked everywhere, but there was just the old mare.
11  I ran out to the truck screamin', "Mama, Mama, where's the
12  pony?" And she's just a standin' there laughin' and holdin'
13  her sides like they was gonna bust open.
14    She says, "Aw son, there ain't no pony! Boy, I lied to
15  you, kinda like you been lyin' to me. Ain't lyin' fun?" Well,
16  boy, I ran straight into the house and into my bedroom. I
17  can still remember lyin' there and just bawlin' my eyes out.
18  I think I felt the deepest disappointment I ever felt in my life.
19  Nah, I mean it. There ain't been nothin' since that hit me so
20  hard as not gettin' that pony. *(Sighs.)* Before I went to sleep
21  that night, Mama came in to tell me that she loved me. And
22  I know she did. And the way she tells it now, that was my
23  cure. Yup. After that day I stopped tellin' those evil fibs that
24  she had tucked away in her pouch and let stew into a nice
25  little lesson. Yep. So, that's Mama alright. If ya wanna
26  understand Mama, ya gotta first understand that she's a
27  real piece of work, just like my dad says. And that, my
28  friends, ain't no lie.

# 6. Double Standard

1    *(On his cell)* **Melissa ... Melissa, wait ... You're not letting**
2    **me tell my side of the story. Melissa.** *(She hangs up on him.)*
3    **Melissa, are you there?** *(Looks at his friend "Zach.")* **She hung**
4    **up on me.** *(Looks at the phone in disbelief.)* **She hung up on**
5    **me. Me. The Homecoming King. The man on campus voted**
6    **"Most Likely to Succeed." What do you think's wrong with**
7    **her? Has she lost her mind? Dude, quit laughing.** *(Looks at*
8    *the phone again.)* **Geez. She wouldn't even let me explain.**
9    **What a ...** *(Shakes his head.)* **She probably thinks I'm gonna**
10   **call her back. Yeah, right. Not in a million years, baby. Dude.**
11   **Quit laughing. This is so not funny. You know how bad this**
12   **could be? Dude, the prom is tomorrow night. If Melissa**
13   **doesn't go with me, I'll have to get a date in** *(Looks at watch)*
14   **twenty-four hours. Twenty-four hours to be exact. Zach,**
15   **come on, if this was a normal twenty-four hour period I'd**
16   **have no problem getting a date. But this is twenty-four**
17   **hours before the prom. Any girl that doesn't have a date by**
18   **now probably isn't worth asking.**

19   *(Looks at the phone.)* **That's it. I'm gonna call her back**
20   **and try one more time.** *(Dials the number.)* **Melissa? Melissa,**
21   **don't hang up. I need to tell you what happened. I need to**
22   **... Melissa?** *(Angry and shouting into the phone)* **Melissa!**
23   *(Looks at "Zach.")* **She did it again. What is the problem here?**
24   **I mean, doesn't she know that any girl at Seymour would kill**
25   **to go out with me? Here she is, monopolizing me for the past**
26   **year. One night, just one night, I go out with another girl**
27   **and she flips. Yeah, well so what if Nora would flip on you**
28   **too. You and Nora might as well be married with four kids**

1 already. You know what I'm saying is true. You're, like, old
2 before your time. But me? I need to be free to explore a
3 *little.*
4 What do you mean, "How would I be if the shoe were on
5 the other foot?" You mean, how would I feel if Melissa went
6 out one time with another guy? Just for fun, right? I would
7 be one hundred percent A-OK with that. I'm cool, dude. I'm
8 understanding. I mean, I might get a little jealous at first,
9 but if she explained it to me, like I was trying to explain to
10 her, I'd be totally cool with it. I'd say "Melissa, you are a
11 beautiful young woman. You have every right to wonder what
12 it's like to date other guys. It's perfectly natural. I love you,
13 so I understand. I forgive you and I think we should move
14 past this thing and go to the freakin' prom!"
15 Huh? A confession to make? Dude, don't tell me you
16 cheated on Nora? You did? No way! Dude, that's awesome.
17 Give me some skin, homeslice. *(Laughs.)* Ah, man. And all
18 this time I thought you were like some old geezer whose
19 eyes never roamed. So who was it? Hey, man, give it up.
20 Who's the babe, do I know her? You want me to guess? OK.
21 Hillary Head. Too bad man. She's hot. Oh, I know, Candace
22 Russell? No. Dude, just tell me! What? What?! Dude, what
23 did you just say? Don't mumble. Say it to my face. You just
24 said Melissa, but I know you don't mean my Melissa, do
25 you. You do? You do?! OK, that solves everything. Thanks a
26 lot. No more Melissa and no more of you. Yeah, I'm leaving
27 dude. You just lost a friend.

# 7. The Talk

1     Hey, gorgeous. I just came by to say good-bye before I
2 leave tomorrow. Man, you are looking better than the first
3 time I laid eyes on you, you know that? I still remember that
4 day. It was my sixteenth birthday. I woke up that morning
5 feeling so bummed. So ... miserable because I had just
6 broken up with that girl from the swim team. Yeah, so there
7 I am moping and thinking it's gonna be a rotten day and
8 then ... lo and behold, the best thing that ever happened to
9 me ... I walked out my front door and laid my eyes on you
10 for the first time, in all your glory. Yeah, that was the best
11 day of my life.

12     You got to understand that, even though we have to say
13 good-bye, nothing has changed. I mean, the way I feel about
14 you hasn't changed. It's just that I've changed. Time just
15 passes and we find ourselves faced with decisions. Forks in
16 the road. Then, when we make a decision to follow a path,
17 like me deciding to go away to college, and our decisions ...
18 they shape us, they ... change us. They change our
19 priorities.

20     So, I know that I always said that it would be you and
21 me forever, but I see now that we're gonna have to be strong
22 and make the break. But look on the bright side, my little
23 brother Timmy is gonna take really good care of you. I know
24 he's only thirteen and can't take you anywhere or anything,
25 but he can still keep an eye on you, you know. He can let
26 me know how you're doing when I call home and stuff. And
27 I will definitely ask about ya, 'cause ... I know I'm gonna
28 miss you. I know you can't tell me this, but I have a big

1  feeling you're gonna miss me too.
2      Just think, one day, when I'm a doctor, or an architect,
3  I'll be married with six kids crammed into a van and I'll think
4  back to you and the good times we had together. Just you
5  and me. And, well, sometimes that girl from the mini mart.
6  Yeah, I'll look back on those carefree days and wonder
7  where you are. Will somebody love you the way I did? Will
8  they take care of you the way I did? Or will you be falling
9  apart? Showing all the wear and tear of a life less sheltered
10  than here at twenty-one-twenty-three Cranberry Lane. *(Hears*
11  *a noise.)* Oh, hey Dad, what's going on? Oh, me? Talking to
12  myself? Nah. Just saying good-bye to old Betsey here. I'm
13  sure gonna miss her, but I'll never forget her. Do you
14  remember your first car, Dad?

# 8. Normal

1     Carol, did you ever wonder what things would be like if
2 our parents were normal? Oh come on, Carol, they are not.
3 Mom and Dad? Get real. You're just too loyal to tell the
4 truth.
5     OK, so I'll tell you why they are not normal parents. Do
6 you ever remember them giving us a bedtime? No. But you
7 do remember Mom waking us up that night to take us on a
8 moonlit walk through the snow at midnight? On a school
9 night. Then the next day she decided to keep us home so
10 that we could write poems and draw pictures all day of what
11 we had seen. So? So, she didn't bother to call the school
12 and tell them we were sick or couldn't come in. We got in
13 trouble for skipping. Remember? We kept asking her to write
14 us a note and she refused because she didn't believe in all
15 that bureaucratic garbage.
16     Come on, Carol, did you at least ever wonder what things
17 would be like if Mom had been a normal mom? We wouldn't
18 be as creative? We wouldn't be free thinkers? Yeah, maybe.
19 But maybe we'd fit in. Yeah, yeah, I know, you don't want to
20 fit in. Well, if that's really true, that's great. But I do. I do
21 want to fit in sometimes. And I can't. I never will. Not here
22 anyway. If Mom and Dad wanted to be such free spirits and
23 free thinkers they should have brought us up some place a
24 little more cosmopolitan. Like New York City. Or how about
25 Paris. Someplace with artists and other crazies and we'd fit
26 in just fine.
27     Yeah, I know artists aren't crazies, but you know. I
28 mean, people like Dad. OK, performance artists. Remember

1 that time Dad dragged our little rowboat downtown and
2 stood in it all day singing "Row, row, row, your boat gently
3 down the stream." Come on, you have to admit that was
4 crazy. Yeah, I know. He wanted to remind the nine-to-fivers
5 that they need to relax. But why did he need to drag me
6 along that day? I hated it. I just kept wishing that he was
7 one of those nine-to-fivers and that I wasn't wearing jeans
8 that were a size too big and had holes in them.
9 *(Sighs.)* Carol, if you don't see that Mom and Dad are not
10 normal parents, then I think that it's only because you're
11 one of them. And that means that somehow I came out
12 being the only member of this family that doesn't fit in. I
13 guess that makes *me* the weird one. *(Laughs.)* I bet you guys
14 sit around talking when I'm not here and Mom says, "Did
15 you ever wonder what things would have been like if Lucas
16 had been a *normal* son?"

# 9. The Room at the End of the Hall

1     I finally got invited over to Dale's house. I mean, it's
2  been two years since we moved here, right? And Dale and I
3  became friends pretty much right off the bat. So that means
4  that for two years we've always hung out at my house. But
5  now I think I understand. He didn't want to talk about his
6  sister.

7     Yesterday he called me and asked me to come over to
8  help him do some stuff in the yard for his dad. After we
9  worked for a while we went inside. His parents weren't there
10  and it was really quiet and dark. None of the curtains were
11  open. We went upstairs to the TV room and watched the
12  game. He had to go downstairs for something and I went out
13  in the hall to find the bathroom. I opened this door at the
14  end of the hall that I thought was it, but it was a bedroom.
15  A girl's bedroom. It had all this paraphernalia from Tucker
16  High and a big picture of a girl and Dale on the wall taken
17  at the Grand Canyon. I was still standing there looking in
18  when Dale came back up. He started freaking out. He's like,
19  "What do you think you're doing? That door is supposed to
20  stay shut!" I tried to explain about the bathroom, but he got
21  so weird that I just left.

22     I went over to Henry's house and told him what
23  happened. Turns out that was Dale's sister's room. Yeah. A
24  couple years before we moved here there was this huge
25  accident one night out on Ritter Lane. Dale's sister and this
26  other girl from out of town had been celebrating one of their
27  birthdays that day. They had started early in the morning
28  and gone house hopping to all their friends. One of their

1 friends had given them a big thermos of some kind of liquor.
2 And by the time that accident happened they were totally
3 drunk I guess. Henry said they think the car was going like
4 eighty miles per hour. They tried to pass somebody and lost
5 control of the car. It exploded in the woods and one of the
6 girls died instantly. Dale's sister? No, she didn't die. She
7 was the driver. She was critically injured, but when she
8 recovered she was charged with vehicular homicide while
9 driving intoxicated. She's serving fifteen years in Bradley.

10 Scary, right? And everyone says she got off easy. So she
11 hasn't been in that room for, like, three years. But Henry
12 says they keep it exactly the way it was when she left it with
13 her pompoms and stuff and her old stuffed animals on the
14 dresser. Nobody in the town talks about it. Out of respect
15 to Dale and his parents. It like devastated them. But who
16 wouldn't be devastated, right? I wonder who gave them that
17 thermos of liquor? Henry says they did an investigation, but
18 they never were sure. Everyone clammed up to protect
19 somebody. And by the time Dale's sister was able to talk to
20 the police, she couldn't remember things clearly. Well,
21 whoever that person is, I think they should come forward
22 and they should have to share a cell with Dale's sister. They
23 should have to spend the next fifteen years thinking about
24 nothing but what happened that night. But then again, they
25 probably do. Right?

# 10. He Just Doesn't Get It

1   All my life I've been helping my dad in his shop. He's a
2   mechanic and we work on cars. Mostly foreign. You know,
3   European, some Japanese. He loves what he does and he
4   loves when we work together. I mean, that's our father and
5   son bonding time. We don't do anything else together really.
6   I mean, like, we don't go fishing or camping, or go to football
7   games and stuff. It's not that he wouldn't do those things if
8   he could. It's just, well, he's always working. And so if I
9   want to spend any time with him I work with him. It's kind
10  of cool, because I'm probably the only teenage guy that I
11  know that could probably open his own European auto shop
12  tomorrow. And I'd be successful too. I know I would.
13      But ya know, the funny thing is, that's not what I want
14  to do with my life. I mean, actually, I kind of hate working
15  on cars. Have I ever told my dad that? No. No, he wouldn't
16  understand. He'd be, ya know, kind of hurt I guess. *(Sighs.)*
17  That's probably a huge understatement, actually. I mean,
18  he'd probably be crushed. That's his dream for me, ya know.
19  That one day I'll take over his shop. Yeah, that's his dream.
20  But that's not mine. I'm not even really sure what my dream
21  is, but I know ... I know that it's not that. I just wish, I
22  mean, I hope that one day I'll get up the nerve to tell him.
23  'Cause, the longer I wait, the bigger the disappointment it's
24  gonna be. For him, ya know. Yeah, he's gonna be *really*
25  disappointed. But if he'd paid attention to who I really am,
26  he wouldn't have to be disappointed. He'd have known for
27  years now. He sees me as who he wants me to be and not
28  who I am. I'm not him. I mean, a son is not put on this earth

1    to carry on his father's own personal dream. It's so obvious

2    to most people that we all have our own dreams, our own

3    ideas, but my dad? He just doesn't get it.

# 11. Paranoia

1     I just like talking about the things that I love to do.
2 Places that I love to be. Surfing, the beach, summers at my
3 grandfather's house. So that's what I talked about. I hope
4 she wasn't bored. I tried to get her to talk about the stuff
5 she loves, but no could do. Maybe she doesn't love to do
6 anything? I find that hard to believe, but it's possible, I
7 guess. So anyway, that's what we talked about. I just about
8 talked her ear off. She probably hated the whole date. She
9 probably thought I was obsessed with myself or something,
10 right? People always say that, but what else am I supposed
11 to talk about? The six o'clock news?

12     Anyway, like I said, I couldn't get her to open up. I
13 mean, I still had a great time, but I guess she probably
14 didn't. Yeah, I'm going to ask her out again for sure. She
15 was really sweet and all that. I mean, first we went to the
16 movies and she said that she didn't care which one we went
17 to. I asked her if she wanted popcorn or anything. She just
18 said, "No thanks." I was really glad because that saved me
19 a wad of cash. But I would have gotten it for her. So then
20 after the movie we went to that burger place at the mall. We
21 both had hamburgers. What else do you get at a burger
22 place? So then that's when I probably talked her ear off.
23 After that I took her home. Hey, I'm not going to tell you
24 every detail of the date. After I took her home, that part is
25 off limits.

26     How soon do you think I should call her? Now? We just
27 went out yesterday. She'll think I'm in love with her or
28 something. What's wrong with that? It might scare her off. I

1 want her to think of me as a friend and sort of let the
2 relationship build from there. She's shy. She'll probably
3 want to take it slow. But on the other hand, if I don't call
4 her right away she might get her feelings hurt.
5      What? She might start dating someone else? You think?
6 Yeah, she is pretty cute. You think she's interested in
7 someone else? You think that's why she didn't have much
8 to say? She was just kind of putting in time with me or
9 something? In that case, I shouldn't call her at all. That's so
10 rude. But you know what, I'll bet that's exactly what's going
11 on here. She's probably got some other guy on the line and
12 maybe he didn't ask her out this weekend or something and
13 she wanted to, I don't know, make him jealous or
14 something. Or not be home when he called. My sister does
15 that stuff all the time. And here I am spilling my guts to her
16 and she's probably sitting there thinking of this other guy
17 and didn't even hear a word I said. Or she heard everything
18 I said and she's busy telling all her friends everything I said
19 and laughing about what a jerk I am. She's probably telling
20 them I talked so much that she couldn't get a word in.
21 Which is a big fat lie. And that's one thing I can't stand. A
22 liar. You know, she can have whoever this guy is that she
23 really wants. I don't know what I was even thinking when I
24 asked her out, but believe me, that won't happen again.

# 12. Jealousy

1     Am I jealous? Yeah. Yeah, of course I'm jealous. Who
2  wouldn't be? My whole life, it's like, he gets everything and
3  I get nothing. So, yeah, I'd say I'm jealous. Jealous to the
4  point of not being able to think about anything else?
5  Sometimes.

6     You see, it's like this. Ever since my little brother was
7  born he's been like this dream come true for my parents.
8  'Cause, well, you know, he's both of theirs. I mean, my
9  stepfather has been really great to me my whole life, but in
10  reality I'm some other man's son. But Damian? He's both of
11  theirs. So it's like they may try to hide it, but he's *their* son.
12  I'm just the other kid in the family. And that means that
13  ever since he was born, they showered stuff on him like you
14  would not believe. When his fifth grade class went to camp
15  in the Keys, Mom let him go. That exact same trip was
16  offered to me when I was in fifth grade, but Mom said no. I
17  got up the nerve to ask her about that one day. I said, "So,
18  how come Damian gets to go and I didn't? What's that
19  about?" She gave me this look and goes, "Patrick, I can't
20  believe you're jealous of your own brother."

21     I wanted to say "Half brother," 'cause I was really
22  irritated at that point. But I remained calm and I said,
23  "Mom, I'm just asking why I didn't get to go."

24     She says, "You know we couldn't afford it back then."
25  And that's true I guess. But I don't think they would have
26  said no to Damian even if money was tight. They would have
27  found a way. Well, it's just like last year. Damian's baseball
28  team needed another chaperone and Mom rescheduled

1  some big meeting at work just so she could go. She never
2  once did that for me. It's like her priorities are like this:
3  Rick, that's my stepfather, Damian, her job, and then me.
4  No, wait a second, I'm leaving her cat off the list. Yum Yum.
5  Yum Yum definitely comes slightly above me on the list, so
6  we don't want to leave her out. So, yeah, anyway, that's why
7  I'm jealous. You'd be jealous, too. Wouldn't you?

# 13. Not Your Everyday Valedictorian

1     Principal Ellis, faculty members, family, friends, and
2 fellow graduates, I am honored to stand here before you
3 today as your valedictorian. Today is a day to look back at
4 four years of high school with nostalgia and to look forward
5 to a future that is for the most part unknown. Some of you
6 probably think you have your future all mapped out. Being
7 the valedictorian and the recipient of a full scholarship to
8 the school of my choice, some of you may think that I have
9 my future mapped out. But in reality, we can only try to
10 steer our future, against a rushing current that is steering
11 us.

12    Yes, that's right, I stand here today to tell you that life
13 will have its own way with us. In high school we have seen
14 that to some degree. Some of us to a great degree. And it
15 isn't only hardships and tragedies that can unexpectedly
16 change our path. Sometimes it is good fortune, or what
17 seems to be good fortune at the time. The good fortune of
18 getting accepted to a good school. The good fortune of
19 meeting the right person, eventually. That soul mate, that
20 one true love that everyone dreams will be there for them.

21    Of course, statistics show us that something like one
22 out of every two marriages end in divorce. So, chances are
23 your soul mate won't really be your soul mate after all. So
24 let's say in about two or three years you meet some
25 fabulous girl or guy and you spend the next ten or fifteen
26 years devoting your life to them and then one day you find
27 out they've been lying to you the whole time and never cared
28 at all, or maybe they thought they cared and now they are

1  all about somebody else. What are you gonna do? You've
2  just wasted what may be about one seventh of your life.
3  Well, that's if you think you'll live to your seventies or
4  eighties. And who knows, maybe you'll get hit by a bus
5  when you're forty. So that means this great girl or guy that
6  you're gonna be so happy you met — let's say your
7  freshman or sophomore year of college — could actually end
8  up wasting about one fourth of your life or more. I mean,
9  let's face it, every graduate sitting in this room is thinking
10 they are not the one that's gonna get hit by the bus. It's
11 gonna be the next guy, right? Well, I'm here to tell you that
12 you just never know.
13    So, my friends, my message today is short and simple,
14 really. Use your time wisely and though you may think
15 you've got it all planned out, we're all in the dark about the
16 future. But don't be afraid. Though we may be in a boat
17 that's slowly sinking, we are all in the same boat. Good
18 luck, best wishes, and as happy as you are right now, may
19 this *not* be the happiest day of your life.

# 14. The King of Monologues

1    How could this happen? How could he get the part? My
2    part! That was supposed to *my part*. Everybody knew it!
3    Everybody! They were all like, "You're gonna be the lead in
4    the school play again this year. That part is so perfect for
5    you." Jane Dozmak even said she thought Mrs. Anderson
6    picked the play because the lead was so right for me! Yeah,
7    Jane. And she's practically Mrs. Anderson's right arm. I
8    just got this weird visual when I said that. You know, Mrs.
9    Anderson reaches out to sign your hall pass or something
10   and Jane *is* her right arm, you know? Hey, that would make
11   a really cool cartoon. You should do that! *(Sighs.)* It must be
12   so easy to be an artist. To draw or paint whatever you want
13   and not have to get someone to give you permission to do
14   your craft.
15       Being an actor can suck sometimes. Well, it's just like
16   this play. I know that I would make a really great Dr.
17   Sanderson, but all the greatness that would have been will
18   never be seen. She must not have liked my monologue.
19   That's just so weird, because everybody in drama considers
20   me the King. The King of Monologues. Yeah, we do them all
21   the time in class and Mrs. Anderson loves mine. I get an A
22   every time. And last year she gave me the lead. So I just
23   don't get it. What happened? He's taller than me. Maybe
24   that's it. No, you artists really do have it made. I'm at the
25   mercy of the director. You're at no one's mercy. How freeing.
26       Yeah, I guess. A one-man show is a possibility. I wonder
27   if there are any out there that would be right for me. What?
28   Write one? Well ... that's a ... hey, that's a possibility. I'm a

1    pretty good writer. Yeah! Who better to right a one-man
2    show than me, the King? You're pretty smart, you know
3    that. I'll write it, direct it, star in it and ... What should it be
4    about? Any ideas?

# 15. The First Date

1      My first date was with this girl who didn't like to talk.
2 She wasn't shy. At least I don't think she was. She just
3 didn't like to speak. It was weird. 'Cause I like to talk. You
4 know me. But — huh? How did we end up on a date? It was
5 a setup. She was visiting my neighbors for the summer. I
6 wanted to go out with her. She was pretty and she seemed
7 sweet. But that date was kind of hard. It's not like I can't
8 go on talking for hours all by myself with no help from
9 anyone, but I sort of wanted to know what she was thinking.
10 If she was thinking. And I never did find out.

11      I've had a few other dates after that, but nothing serious
12 yet. I guess I'm kind of a nerd. I mean, my life pretty much
13 rotates around school, homework, and stuff. I don't usually
14 tell anyone about this, but I spend a lot of time writing. What
15 do I write? Well, I keep a journal for one thing. It's pretty
16 extensive. I don't just write a few lines, like what I did today.
17 I sort of explore my thoughts, discuss current events.

18      The first date? Oh, yeah, I did write about that. It's
19 funny, I wrote this whole imaginary scenario the night
20 before, actually. It was all about this amazing first date that
21 would change my life forever. So, it was pretty anti-climactic
22 when I had to write about the reality the next night. But I'm
23 still glad I wrote about it. When I'm an old fogey of forty-five
24 and just about can't remember my own name anymore, I'll
25 still be able to look back in my journal and remember my
26 first date. And maybe I'll use it in a story one day. Well,
27 yeah, I write fiction too. No, I never tell anyone. I don't know
28 why I'm even telling you. I did tell her that night though. The

1 girl that my neighbors set me up with. Tara. Her name was
2 Tara. No, she wasn't impressed. At least she didn't seem
3 impressed. I couldn't tell. Like I said, she pretty much didn't
4 say two words all night. She's supposedly coming back
5 again next summer. Maybe I'll try again.

# 16. The Breakup

1     Hey, can we go into the other room. I need to talk to you.
2     Privately. I don't know how to tell you this, Sarah. OK. I
3     want to ... I think ... we should ... break up. Don't. Don't get
4     all hysterical. *(Looks around.)* **People will hear you.** *(Loudly)*
5     **Stop screaming!** *(Quietly)* **Shhhh. OK, OK, we won't. We**
6     **won't. We won't break up.** *(Shaking his head)* **Calm down.**

7     OK. We won't break up, but maybe we should talk about
8     the fact that it might happen eventually. Sarah, let's be
9     mature about this. Every time I want to talk about anything
10   serious you start crying. *(Sighs.)* I don't want to hurt you,
11   but I feel like I'm held hostage to your emotions. I care
12   about you too much. That's the problem. And you know
13   that. So when I try to talk about something I think might be
14   the right thing to do ... Don't worry, I won't say it.

15   *(Sighs.)* Anyway, anytime I try to bring up the subject
16   you play on my sympathy, on my caring for you. Good
17   question. If I care about you how could I ever even bring up
18   the subject? Because I care about you, but I'm not sure if
19   I'm in love. Oh geez, here come the tears again. Sarah!
20   Sarah! I'm just not sure, because I haven't dated that many
21   girls. You know what. I probably am madly, deeply in love
22   with you, I just don't have enough experience to know that.
23   And that's why sometimes I think a little experience dating
24   other people might make our relationship even stronger.
25   Eventually. Yeah, so what I'm saying is, I think we should
26   break up so that if we get back together ... OK, *when* we
27   get back together, we'll be one hundred percent sure that
28   it's the right thing. You know, that this is crazy mad love
29   and all that.

1  Stop crying, Sarah. I'm just saying this is something we
2 might want to consider, that's all. I'm not saying we should
3 do anything right now. No, no, no, of course not. No, no, no,
4 we're not breaking up. No. *(Sighs.)* Everything's fine.

# 17. Why?

1    Why or how do we keep on loving our parents even when
2    we start to learn they are only human? That they are flawed?
3    That's what I want to write about. Yeah, that's what my
4    paper is going to be about. How about you? Have you come
5    up with anything?

6    What? What would the world be like if the earth was a
7    cube instead of a globe? Are you serious? How can you
8    possibly write a paper about that? I don't think that's what
9    Mr. Anselm wanted. No, he wanted us to write about the
10   human experience. Yes, of course, living on a planet that
11   had edges would change everything, but that's more of a
12   science fiction essay. I think Mr. Anselm wanted real issues,
13   not "what if" scenarios. OK, so how could you make that a
14   real issue? How does the roundness of the earth impact our
15   day-to-day living? Really? You really want to write about
16   that? Well, when you're done you can probably sell it. Yeah,
17   as an alternative to sleeping pills. Who cares that the earth
18   is round! Are you on something?

19   (Sighs.) OK, whatever. I really don't care what you write.
20   My idea is going to rock. Yeah, the thing about our parents
21   and how, you know, as we grow and mature (Looks at his
22   friend), I take that back, as some of us grow and mature, we
23   look at our parents and we see things that we didn't see
24   when we were five-, six-, or seven-years-old. We see their
25   flaws. Yeah, their flaws. What? You're parents don't have
26   any flaws? Yeah right! You mean you just haven't discovered
27   them yet. Believe me, they've got 'em.

28   Well, for one thing, you're mom is kind of lazy, right?

1  Hey, no offense, but I sort of noticed that she doesn't really
2  do much, does she? And your dad, man, your dad is a nice
3  guy, but he's really not funny. And he thinks he's *really*
4  funny. Yeah, that's a flaw. He has a distorted perception of
5  himself and therefore he subjects others to his lame jokes
6  and thinks that they find them amusing. Hey, don't get
7  mad, I'm just trying to help you see that even though our
8  parents have flaws we love them anyway, right?
9      My parents? Oh, don't worry, I know what my parents'
10 flaws are. My dad, he'll say anything to anyone without
11 thinking first. And my mom, she can be downright insulting.
12 Boy, it's funny that I didn't inherit those traits. I wonder
13 why?

# 18. I Could Have Been Fred Astaire

1     I hate football. No, I'm not just saying that. I really,
2  really hate football. That's really great that you think I'm
3  good at it. I mean, I know I am. But you know what? Just
4  because you're good at something doesn't mean you have to
5  like it. So why do I play? *(Sighs and shrugs his shoulders.)* It's
6  always been the easiest thing to do to please my dad. Oh
7  yeah, my dad *loves* football. He was a quarterback just like
8  me in high school. Yeah, he really loves that I'm on the team
9  and that he can come to all the games and, you know, brag
10  to his friends.
11     What would I rather be doing? I don't know. Well, I mean,
12  yeah, I do know, but it's stupid. You'll think it's stupid. OK,
13  if I tell you this and anyone finds out ... Well, it's kind of
14  embarrassing. It probably shouldn't be, but I just get
15  embarrassed. Why? 'Cause ... I'd rather be tap dancing.
16  Yeah, tap dancing.
17     When I was a kid, my mom used to take me and my
18  sister to all these old movies. You know, musicals. There
19  was this little theatre down the street from our apartment
20  that always showed these really old musicals. You know, like
21  Gene Kelly stuff and Fred Astaire. So I used to come home
22  and try out these dance numbers. I was really good. I mean,
23  you think I'm good at football, but, um, tap dancing ... I was,
24  you know, kind of a natural. So, anyway, my mom bought
25  me tap shoes and got me some lessons. I had to take the
26  bus downtown to get to the place. It was called Ginnie's
27  School of Dance. I had to walk past a bunch of the kids in
28  the neighborhood to get to the bus stop and I always hid my

1 tap shoes. Yeah, tap dancing wasn't the coolest thing to
2 them, like it was to me.
3     One day, some kid from school came to pick up his
4 sister from dance class and he saw me there. I was standing
5 there with my tap shoes on and I remember feeling like such
6 a jerk. I went home and told my mom that I didn't want to
7 take lessons anymore. She didn't question it. I put my
8 shoes under my bed and the next time I took them out, it
9 was, like, two years later. They didn't even fit anymore.
10 Funny, huh? I could have been another Fred Astaire.

# 19. Unconditional Love

1     Everybody always talks about unconditional love like it's
2 the greatest thing in the world, but I completely disagree. To
3 love someone unconditionally is to say that they can walk all
4 over you, stab you in the back, and you'll still love them.

5     That just doesn't work for me. I think love needs to be
6 a two-way street, a give-and-take. There should be ground
7 rules for any relationship, and the first rule should be that
8 you get back the love you give. I think that is the basis for
9 any healthy relationship. People just use that unconditional
10 love garbage to get away with stuff, to treat you like dirt,
11 and to ruin your self-esteem.

12     Just think about it. Somebody tells you over and over
13 how much they love you and then every once in a while they
14 call you names, or lie to you, or take your stuff without
15 asking and then destroy it. It makes your self-esteem sink
16 to the bottom, right? 'Cause somewhere inside your head
17 you've got to be thinking, "Wow, this person loves me and
18 they still treat me this way? I must be worthless."

19     Yeah, I think that's what happens. So, no, I don't accept
20 the unconditional love theory. Love definitely has conditions
21 and let me tell you, actions speak louder than those three
22 little words. I say don't tell me that you love me unless you
23 mean it. And you don't mean it if you intentionally hurt me
24 over and over again. And that goes for family too, as far as
25 I'm concerned. I mean, I'm just lucky because my family is
26 all about treating each other with respect and love. You
27 know, thinking before we speak, considering each other's
28 feelings. That's just how I was brought up. But I see my

1 friends that don't have families like that and I guess it's
2 easy for me to say all this because I'm the fortunate one. I
3 don't have to walk in their shoes.
4      But really, how far does unconditional love have to go?
5 How much does somebody have to take before they stop
6 loving someone or believing that someone loves them?
7 Maybe it's just a matter of understanding the difference
8 between love and attachment, or love and loyalty. I don't
9 know. It's really complex. But for me, I say love is as love
10 does.

# 20. A Simple Life

1     My older brother was always afraid of heights, but from
2    the time he was about seven he knew that he wanted to be
3    a pilot — everyone teased him, including our dad. Dad used
4    to get us to help him around the house and when Tom was
5    afraid to go up on the ladder or to the roof, Dad would make
6    fun of him. He'd say, "The pilot is afraid to go up on a
7    ladder?" The other kids would make fun of him too because
8    they saw that it was OK with Dad. I always knew that Tom
9    wanted to prove them all wrong. And there was something
10   else I knew that made everything harder. For some crazy
11   reason I was always Dad's favorite. I hated that and I could
12   never figure out why. I didn't have Tom's fear of heights, but
13   it wasn't that. Maybe because I came along at a different
14   time in his life. Or maybe because I didn't remind him of
15   himself. Tom was the spitting image of Dad, you see.
16   Well, when Tom turned eighteen and graduated from
17   high school, I was so proud that he joined the Air Force.
18   Tom went through the fire to become a pilot and even then,
19   Dad didn't acknowledge it. Why do we make life so complex?
20   Shouldn't it be easy? Today they are bringing my brother
21   Tom's body home. He was shot down in combat. He's a
22   hero. My dad is devastated. He hasn't stopped crying. And
23   I know why. He's full of nothing but regrets. It's so simple,
24   really. If only people would catch on. You can't hurt anyone
25   without hurting yourself. For every time my dad made Tom
26   suffer, he has to suffer now. It's as simple as that. A very
27   simple equation really. A simple life.

# 21. Self-Fulfilling Prophecy

1    *(DEREK enters study hall and sits next to "Felicia.")* **Hey, I**
2  **was beginning to think he was never going to leave.** *(Looks*
3  *at his watch.)* **Do you know what time it is? Yeah, well, he**
4  **may have a geometry exam tomorrow, but we have a dinner**
5  **date tonight. Is he going to pay you for the extra time?**
6  **You're too nice. You made a deal and he should stick to it.**
7  **Ten dollars an hour. He ran over by twenty minutes. He**
8  **needs to give you three dollars and thirty three cents. No,**
9  **make that three dollars and thirty four cents. Why should**
10  **you get ripped off for a penny just because he can't divide**
11  **ten dollars into three parts equally? What do you mean "I'm**
12  **getting weird?" I'm just ...** *(Pauses.)* **He likes you. I said** *he*
13  *likes you.* **Oh, come on, that's bologna. You may think it's**
14  **a tutor-tutee relationship, or whatever you call it, but he's**
15  **thinking of some other kind of tooting. Oh, yes he is. You**
16  **can't tell me that he really didn't get the whole hypotenuse**
17  **thing down in an hour. He really needed that extra twenty**
18  **minutes? I'll tell you what he needed. He needed to sit close**
19  **to you and smell your hair. Yeah, your hair. It smells like**
20  **peaches.**

21    *(Moves close and takes a whiff.)* **Oh, please, Mrs. Carter is**
22  **not watching. Yeah, she's looking this way, but that doesn't**
23  **matter. She can't see a thing. She just puts that disgusted**
24  **look on her face in case anybody's doing anything wrong.**
25  **And probably about ninety-nine percent of the time**
26  **somebody in here** *is* **doing something wrong, so she's a**
27  **pretty smart lady when you think about it.**

28    **But I digress. The point is, he likes you and ... I don't**

1 think you should tutor him anymore. What? Me? Possessive?
2 I am not being possessive. I'm being proactive. You see, this
3 is how it all starts. Two people innocently meet in study hall
4 to go over hypotenuses and the next thing you know it's a
5 lesson in, ya know, chemistry. And I don't want that to
6 happen. I don't want to walk in here one day to pick you up
7 for dinner and have you turn to me and say, well, that you're
8 breaking up with me to go out with that loser. Well, that's a
9 really good question. If he's such a loser then why would you
10 choose him over me? I don't know. Felicia, I don't know the
11 answer to that question. But I don't want to find out.
12     Look, it's like this, you're innocent. Yes, you are. I mean,
13 I'm, like, your first real boyfriend, right? OK, there was that
14 guy at camp, but what I mean is, well, like, he doesn't count
15 'cause you guys didn't break up. I mean, camp just ended
16 and you went your separate ways. So it's like you are totally
17 inexperienced at break ups and how they can just happen
18 out of the blue. I, on the other hand, am a veteran. I mean,
19 it's not that I'm a reject and have been dumped a bunch of
20 times, but, hey, I'm older than you and ... Yeah, only by a
21 few months, but when you're our age, believe me, a few
22 months is a really long time. It's like dog years, ya know. So
23 like in teen time, a few months can be like a couple of years.
24 Especially when you're talking heartache and break up and
25 ... Felicia, I just don't want it to happen to us. So, take my
26 word for it. Based on my experience, this whole geometry gig
27 is spelling disaster for us with a capital D. It may not be
28 evident to you right now, but — What? Ah ha, so you are
29 beginning to see the light. And ... what's that? It's over?
30 You're breaking up with me?
31     *(He watches "Felicia" as she gets up and walks away. To*
32 *himself)* **Was I right, or was I right?** *(Calls after her loudly.)*
33 **Felicia, you can't say I didn't warn you!** *(Then quietly)* **Oh,**
34 **sorry, Mrs. Carter.**

# 22. Go Ahead and Cry

1     It was pretty cool. The counselor was nice. She was
2 young and pretty, actually. So that was cool, but also kind
3 of intimidating. You know, talking about all this stuff that's
4 been on my mind and my parents and all that stuff. Yeah,
5 my parents and dealing with all the arguments and the way
6 my dad treats my mom. Bad. He treats her really ... he's
7 really mean. It's like he doesn't respect her. She puts up
8 with it ... but it wears on her. It's been like this for as long
9 as I can remember and I think, at first, she managed, but
10 now it doesn't seem like she's coping too well. It worries
11 me.
12     Yeah, I've talked to her about it. It's weird. All she does
13 is defend him. She says there are reasons why he is the way
14 he is. He had a really hard childhood and then he got
15 married really young. Not to my mom, but to some other
16 lady, and there was this terrible accident and she died. So
17 my mom's theory is that my dad's anger is really just his
18 way of dealing with all this pent up sadness and pain. And
19 according to her, that's why we have to be understanding.
20 That's why it's OK for him to treat her like a child. Yeah, he
21 treats her like a child. He yells at her for one thing. He yells
22 at her the way a parent shouldn't even be allowed to yell at
23 a child. She just puts up with it though. He makes her feel
24 like she's about two inches tall and she just ... lets him.
25     Me? Oh, yeah, he yells at me too. A lot. But I'm pretty
26 good at tuning it out. You know, my counselor said that my
27 mom is probably right about the pain turning into hostility
28 and all that, but she said it's not an excuse. She said that

1 he's an adult and he should realize that his actions are
2 wrong and that he should be the one seeking counseling.
3 She said he needs to accept the responsibility for making a
4 change. I wanted to say, "Fat chance." But I just agreed.
5 She actually suggested that I try to talk to my dad about it
6 and how I feel and all. Then I was thinking, "*Big fat chance!*"
7 But I was like, "OK, I'll try."
8    She said it might help if we did some role playing and so
9 we did. It was kind of interesting, I guess. I didn't say much
10 though. It was weird. It's hard to talk to my dad even when
11 you're just pretending he's there. I thought about it later
12 though. I thought about what I would say to him if I could.
13 And actually, what I would say if I could is a lot more
14 compassionate than I realized. I mean, when all is said and
15 done, I love my dad. I just wish we could all be happy. I wish
16 he never had to go through all that pain and we never had
17 to get the short end of the stick because of it. Or that he
18 had a better way of dealing with the pain. My counselor said
19 it would help if he could just embrace the pain and let
20 himself really feel it for a while. He's probably tried to
21 suppress it. You know, the whole stigma about a guy crying
22 and all that. I've been thinking about that and I think that's
23 probably true. Maybe if he could just spend some time
24 grieving and letting himself feel the pain it would help. So
25 yeah, if there's one thing that I could say to my dad I know
26 what it would be. I'd say, "Dad, it's OK. Go ahead and cry."

# 23. The Dream

1   I had this dream last night about her. It was so real. She
2   was sitting on a bench in front of the library. I came and sat
3   next to her and held her hand. She was so sweet to me. She
4   even said my name. She said, "Jonathan, don't think I don't
5   notice you, because I do."
6       She squeezed my hand and I started to kiss her cheek,
7   but she moved it away. "Don't," she said. I said, "Why?"
8   And she said, "I want you to realize that we're not meant to
9   be. I want you to stop hoping and dreaming that we can ever
10  be together. I want you to get on with your life and start
11  thinking about other girls." I was sitting there crying. I was
12  wiping my face, but I didn't care who saw me. I was just
13  sitting there crying my eyes out. And that was it. That was
14  the whole dream. But it was so real. So ... deep. And it was
15  the first time that I dreamed of her since ... you know, the
16  accident. I kept wondering when I would. *Wishing* that I
17  would. Just to get a chance to see her again.
18      The thing that I keep trying to figure out is what she said
19  at first. "Don't think I don't notice you, because I do." You
20  know, when I first had a crush on her, she acted like she
21  didn't even know that I existed. And later, when we got
22  together, I asked her about it and she said that she really
23  hadn't paid much attention to me, but then she got a
24  chance to know me better when we became partners in
25  chemistry. So it's like my mind was going back to that time
26  before, when she didn't seem to know if I was, you know ...
27  *(Sighs)* dead or alive.
28      Life. It's so strange. I wonder if dreams are just dreams?
29  Or another dimension of reality?

# 24. Who Is That Masked Man?

1   My dad is the most popular teacher at West High. Yep.
2   Kids love him. And he loves them. I've seen him with them
3   in the halls. He's funny, he's kind, he goes the extra mile to
4   make sure they feel like he's connected with them, that he
5   cares. I look at him and I ask myself, why isn't he this way
6   with me? The guy that he is at school, he's certainly not the
7   father that I know. He comes in the door at night and he's
8   tired from a day of caring and as he crosses that threshold,
9   he hasn't an iota of caring left for me. He finds my
10  conversation dull at the dinner table and has told me so
11  repeatedly. So now we rarely talk. In fact, we rarely sit at the
12  dinner table anymore. I think it's because I remind him of
13  my mother. When he's at school, he can forget and live in
14  this happy world, but when he comes home, it's just me.
15  She's gone and I'm the reason. In his mind, at least. She
16  didn't like to be tied down. She didn't like the domestic life.
17  And maybe she didn't like me. That makes me a real loser,
18  doesn't it? First she left me and now he doesn't love me.
19  Well, I shouldn't even say that, because maybe deep down
20  every parent has to love their own kid. But hey, he sure
21  doesn't like me. *That* I'm one hundred percent certain of. For
22  a long time I tried to find ways to make him like me.
23      He teaches English, so I tried to write. I wrote poetry. I
24  wrote some short stories. I even entered a writing contest
25  that I found in a magazine, and miraculously, I won. After he
26  read the story that I'd submitted and won with, he said he'd
27  never pick up a copy of that magazine again. He said that I
28  couldn't write my way out of a paper bag and that by

1   choosing my story for first place they had completely lost
2   his respect. The next day in school I stood outside of his
3   room during class change. His door was open and I heard
4   him talking to this guy about his research paper. He was so
5   encouraging and kind and he kept making the kid laugh. I
6   had to poke my head in the door just to make sure it was
7   really my dad. And sure enough, it looked like my dad. But
8   I know it wasn't him. Who is that masked man?

# 25. Here I Sit

1    *(Sitting at the computer typing. Stops to count words.)*
2    **Twenty-five.** *(Looks at the audience.)* **Oh my gosh! Only nine**
3    **hundred and seventy-five words to go! Argh! I hate Mrs.**
4    **Lowenstein.** *(Looks out the window.)* **It's a beautiful day out**
5    **there and here I sit.** *(Stares at the computer. Types a little bit*
6    *more. Counts again.)* **Forty.** *(Sighs.)* **Only nine hundred and**
7    **sixty more words to go.**
8    *(Looks out the window. Looks at his cell phone and decides*
9    *to pick it up. Dials.)* **Hey man, what's up? Ah, nothing. Where**
10   **are you? At the beach? Nice. Who's there? She is? Aw, man!**
11   **No, I'm not coming. I can't. Mrs. Lowenstein. Yeah, that**
12   **stupid thousand-word essay. Nah, I won't be done any time**
13   **soon. Forty. I've got forty words. Yeah. OK, dude. Later.**
14   *(Puts the phone down. Types again. Stops and counts.)* **Fifty-**
15   **two. That's** *(Has to think about it for a minute)* **only nine**
16   **hundred and forty-eight more words to go. Argh!**
17   *(Cell phone rings. Picks it up.)* **Yo! Hey, man, whazzup?**
18   **Dude!** *(Excited)* **You do! For when?** *(Disappointed)* **I can't. I**
19   **can't go today, man. Nope. Mrs. Lowenstein. Yup, that**
20   **stupid essay. Yeah, man. Nah, I didn't do it last night. I**
21   **watched a movie. Nah, man. I have to do it today. Yeah, me**
22   **too, man. OK. Yeah. Later.** *(Puts the phone down. Scratches*
23   *his head, staring at the computer. Sighs. Types a few more words.*
24   *Looks out the window. To the audience)* **Why can't it rain? I**
25   **mean, at least it could be lousy weather or something? This**
26   **is probably the nicest day we've had all year.** *(Types a few*
27   *more words. Looks at the audience.)* **Maybe I just shouldn't do**
28   **it. Maybe I just shouldn't even graduate. When you think**

1   about it, who really needs a high school diploma? I mean,
2   there are a lot of old billionaires out there that you read
3   about that never graduated from high school. And then
4   there are actors who are like twelve that are making a
5   million bucks. They don't have a high school diploma, now
6   do they?
7       *(Types a few more words and counts.)* **Seventy-five.** *(Types*
8   *again. Then to no one)* **Mrs. Lowenstein, why are you doing**
9   **this to me? Why are you making me write an essay that**
10  **you're probably not even going to read when it's done? I**
11  **mean, seriously, why would you want to read it? It's like**
12  **three weeks till summer vacation starts and you've got a**
13  **life, right?** *(Thinks about it for a minute. Looks at the audience*
14  *and sighs.)* **She'll read it.**
15      *(Types a few more words. Hears his stomach growl. To the*
16  *audience)* **Did you hear that? That was my stomach! Man,**
17  **I'm hungry. Mom! Mom!** *("She" comes in the room.)* **Do we**
18  **have anything to eat? I'm starving. I can't. I can't get up**
19  **from this chair until I finish my essay. That's what you said**
20  **this morning, right? So my question is, does the prisoner**
21  **get to eat? If I die of starvation, will Mrs. Lowenstein be held**
22  **accountable? Cool! Yeah, grilled cheese sounds awesome.**
23  *(Puppy dog face)* **Thanks, Mom. I wuv you!** *(Looks at audience.*
24  *Looks at the computer and counts.)* **Only eight hundred and**
25  **seventy-five more words to go.**

# 26. Halfway

1    I'm halfway done with everything. Halfway done with the
2  lawn. Halfway done with my laundry. Halfway done with my
3  homework. And halfway done with the weekend too. When
4  am I ever gonna be done with all my work before the
5  weekend's over? Just call me "Half Done." But seriously. I
6  didn't even give you the full list. I'm halfway done with
7  washing the cars. Halfway done with cleaning the pool.
8  Halfway done with feeding the dog. No, just kidding, that
9  one's one hundred percent done. But he's still hungry. Every
10 time I walk into the kitchen he's right behind me with his
11 tail wagging.

12    Yup. It seems like everybody, even the dog, wants
13 something out of me. Well, there's that lightbulb in the
14 kitchen that Mom needs me to replace. Dad left me a list of
15 stuff to do in the garage. Peter's failing geometry and
16 somehow that's my fault. We're supposed to "sit together
17 and get him caught up this weekend" according to Mom.
18 Yeah, right. I'm supposed to catch him up on six months of
19 work. Yeah, I said that to her, but she just said, "Toby, he's
20 your *brother* for goodness sake."

21    Yeah, my life is just a long, long list of things to do and
22 not one of them is any fun. But does anybody care? Noooo.
23 *(Sighs.)* They all think I've got it soooo good 'cause I don't
24 have a job. Yeah, right. You know, I'd rather have a job.
25 Then that would be my excuse. "I can't, I'm working this
26 weekend." Or, "I can't, I'm late for work." That's what my
27 sister Marissa does. And she has fun at work too. She's
28 always like, "Oh, the cutest guy came in to the shoe store

1 the other day." Or "Yesterday was so slow I spent the whole
2 day on the phone with Betty."
3     No, my parents aren't fair. They won't let me get a job
4 because I've got to focus on school. I'm the one who has a
5 chance at a scholarship so I couldn't possibly jeopardize
6 that with a job at some fast food joint or pizza delivery gig.
7 But that doesn't stop them from loading up the list of stuff
8 to do around the house. And that's why I'm always halfway
9 done.
10     And if I don't get a scholarship to college, they'll look at
11 me and shake their heads and say, "You didn't get a
12 scholarship, son, even though we supported you all the way
13 through high school and never asked you to even get a part-
14 time job to help out." Yeah, that's exactly what they'll say.
15 I can just hear it. I'd bet you a million dollars ... if I had that
16 much money.

# 27. The Invasion

1    I hate the holidays. Every holiday at my house there's an
2    invasion of all the relatives. And I mean *every* holiday. And
3    it's not really just one set of family relatives. It's two,
4    because my mom remarried three years ago. So, yeah, three
5    years ago, that was the first phase of the invasion. My
6    mom's new husband, my stepdad, has three daughters. So,
7    my brother and I had to give up the luxury of having
8    separate rooms and give one up for them. They weren't too
9    thrilled about three to a room, so I can't say they got it any
10   better than us, but believe me, adding three girls to your
11   household overnight definitely changes things up a bit.

12       Then, like I said, every holiday the relatives, from both
13   sides mind you, pop in or pretty much move in, depending
14   on the holiday and the time they could get off of work, or the
15   rough winter they're having up north. Some of them aren't
16   so bad. But some of them drive me crazy. Some of them
17   make me cringe. And sometimes it's not them, it's just me.
18   I just need some space, you know? The other night I was in
19   the bedroom doing my homework but I really wanted to go
20   outside and take a walk. But I knew that I'd have to walk
21   through the family chat down memory lane that was taking
22   place in the living room. Nanna Harris was going through old
23   photos and was busy telling Linny and Moses about how I
24   made the cutest Halloween costume one year and won fifty
25   bucks at the community center. I knew that I'd have to stop
26   and chat or I'd be rude. So I just stayed put in my room.

27       I wish I could just build a tunnel from my room to the
28   backyard. An escape route. I could climb out the window,

1   but I tried that once and almost got stuck. I wouldn't want
2   to have the story of how I got stuck in the window go the
3   rounds of the relatives for the next couple of years. So,
4   anyway, this holiday is no different than any other. And I
5   hate it. I know, I sound like an antisocial jerk, but hey, you
6   know what, I guess I am.

# 28. Be Afraid, Be Very Afraid

1     Carrie is very jealous. If I had to choose one thing about
2    her that annoys me, it would be that. Her jealousy. Well, for
3    instance, if we go to the mall, and let's say I accidentally
4    look at another girl, she goes ballistic. I mean, at first, I
5    thought it was kind of funny, but now it really gets on my
6    nerves. Or say we're at a restaurant and the waitress is
7    being super friendly, Carrie will say something like, "Why is
8    she flirting with you right in front of me? Who does she think
9    she is?" The poor girl is just doing her job and trying to be
10   nice, but if I give her even so much as a smile, Carrie won't
11   speak to me for the rest of the night. The funny thing is, in
12   all these cases, like the girls at the mall, or the friendly
13   waitresses, Carrie has absolutely nothing to worry about.
14   And I tell her that. She always says, "I'm just afraid of
15   losing you." And I, of course, assure her that there is
16   nothing, absolutely nothing, to be afraid of.
17     But last night ... last night was different. Last night, we
18   went to the hospital to visit Carrie's little brother Tommy. He
19   had his tonsils taken out yesterday and the whole family
20   was there. Poor little guy was looking all pale and skinny in
21   his hospital gown and crying 'cause his throat hurt and all.
22   Carrie walked down the hall to the gift shop with her mom
23   to see if they had anything that might cheer him up.
24     While they were gone, this candy striper walked in. You
25   know, one of those volunteers that work in the pediatrics
26   ward to cheer the little kids up. Well, she walked in and had
27   the sweetest smile and the sweetest personality. She made
28   Tommy smile in about two seconds, left him a really neat

1   little toy that he could play with the next day, and tucked
2   him in really nicely before she smiled at me and walked
3   away. She wasn't all that gorgeous or anything and she was
4   wearing this silly candy striper uniform that wasn't exactly
5   the most flattering, so when she and Carrie crossed paths
6   as she was leaving and Carrie and her mom were coming
7   back from the gift shop, Carrie didn't even notice her. She
8   came in and held my hand and said, "Visiting hours are
9   over, we'll have to come back tomorrow, Tommy." I said,
10  "Yeah, we'll be back tomorrow, kid." We left the hospital,
11  but afterwards I couldn't stop thinking about that candy
12  striper and her sweet smile. I'm going back to the hospital
13  tomorrow night, and if that girl is there again, well ... I have
14  some advice for my jealous girlfriend. Be afraid. Be very
15  afraid.

# 29. Student Director

1     I know it's hard for you to take direction from another
2  kid, but you have to remember that this isn't easy for me
3  either. But *I have to give direction.* That's my job! I am the
4  student director for this play. I'm not trying to boss you
5  around or ... hey, mimicking me is not going to help this
6  situation ... Yeah, you were. I saw you. It's not funny guys.
7  *(Starts to walk away and then turns back.)* Look, do you want
8  to do this show or not? Yeah, well so do I, so we have to
9  make this work.

10  *(Sighs. Looks at his watch.)* We've wasted a half hour
11  already. Let's just go to the scene in the math class. You
12  know what, let's *just* work on the scene in the math class.
13  Everybody else can leave for today. Yeah, go ahead, we'll
14  start back up with scene one tomorrow. Quietly, please!
15  Trisha, Robert, and Tom, please take your places for the
16  math class scene. *(To the students leaving rehearsal)* Yeah,
17  yeah, you guys, see you tomorrow, same time. Quietly,
18  please. *(Looks after them, annoyed. Now to the actors in the*
19  *scene.)* OK, I did some thinking about this scene last night
20  and I think we really need to put a little umph into it. Yeah,
21  umph. No offense, but you guys are just kind of saying your
22  lines with no motivation or anything at this point. And no,
23  no, no, that's my fault. Well, I mean, that's my job, right?
24  To help you find your motivation.

25     OK, so alright, let's start with Tom, who's sitting in the
26  desk at the end of the row. We know that he's asking Trisha
27  for help, right, but she just blows him off and practically
28  ignores him. Then she's super helpful to Robert, who's

1 sitting across from her, asking if he got the notes from the
2 other day and all that stuff, right? Well, we just need to add
3 a little romance here, a little flirtation. Good idea, right?
4 Yeah, I think so too.
5    OK, so now let's take the scene from the top and this
6 time when Tom asks Trisha for help, no, no, no, even before
7 he speaks to her, as the scene opens, we see Tom admiring
8 Trisha from behind. Maybe you could kind of play with a lock
9 of her hair until she sort of notices and thinks it's a bug or
10 something and brushes it away. Trisha, you could drop your
11 pencil and Tom could jump up to get it and you can kind of
12 look annoyed. Yeah, annoyed. 'Cause see, you're in love with
13 Robert, who's sitting next to you. Yeah, in love. That's your
14 motivation for trying to help him out and everything. Trying
15 to find a reason to talk to him when you ask him about the
16 notes. And this time when you do that, when you ask him
17 about the notes, try to say his name like you're being
18 flirtatious. I was thinking of this last night when I couldn't
19 sleep. You could be like, Raaaawbert. You know, kind of
20 draw the name out a little bit and put a little melody behind
21 it. Raaaawbert. Like a little affectionate nickname almost,
22 right? Yes! That's it exactly. OK, OK, this is going to be
23 exciting. Let's take it from the top. Places. Lights up.
24 Action!
25    *(Watches them for a moment, kind of pantomiming,*
26 *mimicking what they're doing.)* Cut! No, no, no. That's not
27 what I meant at all. *(Sighs.)* Tom, get up for a second. Yeah,
28 get up. Look, you stand over there and watch. It's like this.
29 You're sitting here playing with her hair, just very lightly.
30 No, that's not what you were doing. You were practically
31 giving her a scalp massage. Yeah, you were. And Trisha,
32 you're not supposed to be finding it amusing at all. Well, you
33 sure looked like you were. You were all giggly and smiling.
34 Well, try not to be so ticklish.
35    *(Sighs.)* OK, let's try this one more time and maybe we

1 can get it right. Places, please. OK, lights up. Action!
2 *(Watches them, mimics their actions, and mouths their lines,*
3 *then)* Cut, cut, cut! Trisha, what happened to Raaaawbert?
4 No, you didn't. You did not. You said Robert. Yeah, ya did.
5 Look, Trisha, don't argue with me. Just play your
6 motivation, OK? Let's do it one more time. And Robert,
7 when she's talking to you, you should kind of blow her off
8 just the way she blows off Tom. Yeah, because it's like Tom
9 likes Trisha who couldn't care less and Trisha likes Robert
10 who couldn't care less. Get it? OK, good. Let's do this one
11 last time and then we're out of time for today. Ready?
12 Places. Lights up. Action!

# 30. The Weekend

1    It's the weekend again. Whoop-de-do. Ever since Cindy
2  and I broke up, the weekends are ... just like any other day.
3  No, I take that back. The weekends are worse than any
4  other day. Yeah, worse. They just remind me that we're not
5  together anymore. I know, I know, I was the one who broke
6  up with her. And I know it was the right thing to do. I guess.
7  I just didn't realize how *used* to her I was. I mean, we did
8  everything together. We were like inseparable for three
9  years. But you know what, it's time for college, I just ... I
10  know that I want to date other girls. That's all. I mean, high
11  school romances are just that — high school romances. It's
12  not like you're gonna start dating someone when you're
13  fifteen and then just keep on dating them for the rest of
14  your life or until you get married or something. Yeah, sure,
15  your parents did that. Mine too. That's the point. You can
16  see how crazy that was, right? Just look at our parents. No,
17  no, I know I did the right thing.

18    It's just hard. And the fact that she can't be mature
19  about this makes it even harder. She won't even speak to
20  me. No, I don't call her or anything, but you know, I've run
21  into her a couple times around town. She acts like she
22  doesn't even know me. You know what happened last
23  weekend? I went to Andy's to get a pint of vanilla to take
24  home for my mom. Andy's, as you know, used to be Cindy's
25  and my favorite place for ice cream. Yeah, we went there at
26  least once every weekend. Sometimes twice in one day.
27  Yeah, Cindy loves ice cream. So, anyway, I don't go there
28  much anymore 'cause it kind of makes me sad and all that,

1   but last weekend my mom wanted a pint of vanilla so I
2   stopped at Andy's on my way home from school. I go in, get
3   in line, order my pint. I'm standing there waiting and who
4   should walk in, but Cindy. She's with some guy I've never
5   seen before and they're like holding hands and kissing and
6   ... She looks over at me, and it was like she just looked
7   right through me, you know? It was like I wasn't even there.
8   It was *so weird*. I mean, it's like I could still see us standing
9   there in line. Together. Man, I felt like ... *(Sighs.)* Man, I hate
10 the weekends. That's all.

# 31. The Prom or the Tires

1    When I woke up yesterday, I thought it was a typical day.
2  Everything seemed normal. The birds were singing in the
3  trees. The clouds were drifting overhead as I rode my bike
4  to the corner store. It was just like old times, before I got
5  my car.
6    But then my cell rang. It was the tire shop. They figured
7  that I really needed four new tires and the cost was going to
8  be astronomical. I called my mother right away, because I'm
9  a little bit low on the funds these days if ya know what I
10  mean. So I said, "Hi, Ma," in my sweetest, helpless little boy
11  voice. She wasn't in the best of moods apparently. She was
12  like, "Whadya want, Timmy?" She sounded kind of like a
13  bear. So I was like, "Gee, Ma, if this is a bad time, we can
14  talk later." She was like, "Timmy, stop messin' around.
15  Whadya call me for? I don't have time to waste, I'm payin'
16  the bills." I kind of cringed. This was really bad timing. My
17  ma hates to pay the bills. She puts it off and puts it off and
18  then she sits there swearin' and cursin' the day she was
19  born. (Sighs.) Yep, it was really bad timing, 'cause I need
20  those tires for prom night, which is bearing down on me like
21  a fly on my nose.
22    Yep, prom night is only a week away. And Becky has her
23  dress and everything. So here I am, finding out just
24  yesterday that I need four brand new tires. So I just said it,
25  "Ma, I need four new tires on the Impala." At first she didn't
26  say a thing. I thought maybe she had a heart attack and
27  keeled over, but then I heard this growl. No, it was more like
28  thunder. She was like, "Timmy, you can't have four new

1    tires *and* go to the prom. Yer gonna have to choose. Do you
2    want to go to the prom or have new tires on your car so that
3    you can get around all summer long?"
4        I thought about it for a minute. I thought about Becky in
5    her hot, sexy gown waiting for me in her living room. Her dog
6    Missy wagging her tail and just wondering when I was gonna
7    arrive. Then I'd show up and I'd be wearing my jeans and
8    old T-shirt and I'd be like, "Hey Becky!" And I'd give old
9    Missy a holler too. Then she'd say, "Well, gee, Timmy, didn't
10  ya rent a tux?" And I'd be just a chucklin' away. "Heck no,"
11  I'd say, "Who needs a tux when you've got four shiny new
12  tires? Come on out and see." She'd come running out to the
13  car and be like, "Wow, those sure are beautiful tires! Do we
14  have to go to the prom, Timmy? Can't we just go for a ride
15  on those brand spankin' new tires of yours?" And I'd be like,
16  "Funny you should suggest that, Becky, 'cause we aren't
17  going to the prom at all. Get out of that silly old gown and
18  put on your shorts. I didn't even buy tickets to the prom, so
19  we are all set!" Then of course she goes running off into the
20  house just giggling and laughing with Missy running behind
21  wagging her tail.
22      Yep, that was a really good fantasy. But my glazed-over
23  eyes came back into focus and I wiped the sweat off my
24  forehead and called back the tire shop. "Sounds really great,
25  but I think I'd rather ride my bike this summer," I said. You
26  know, it won't be too bad. It'll be just like old times. I'm
27  sure Becky's dad will drive us to the prom and this summer
28  I'll get to know the old neighborhood on my bike, just the
29  way I used to know it. I know what you're thinking. Well,
30  you're probably thinking two things. One, you're thinking,
31  why doesn't this lazy guy just get a job? Answer is I've
32  tried. There just aren't any jobs around here right now. And
33  so many people are out of work that you can't even find
34  anybody who wants you to mow their lawn or anything. But
35  who knows, maybe times will get better and things will

1  improve. The other thing you're probably thinking is, is she
2  really worth it? Becky? Well, I've known Becky since first
3  grade and that is the one thing that I am sure of. She's
4  worth it. She's as good as gold.

# 32. I Know

1    I know everything there is to know about Miley
2  Shephard. Since the sixth grade we've been in the same
3  home room together. That's five years. Five years that I've
4  not only been in the same home room with her, but I've sat
5  directly behind her the whole time. Lucky for me that my
6  last name is Shetfield. And no matter what new kid came
7  into the class throughout the years, it was pretty impossible
8  to wedge anybody between Shephard and Shetfield.
9    So, yup, I know everything there is to know about that
10  girl. I know how she felt when she first got her braces. I was
11  there when they called her to the office the day her dad died.
12  I loaned her lunch money about a thousand times. And I
13  would have never cared if she hadn't paid me back. You see,
14  I'm in love with Miley Shephard. I think I have been since the
15  first day I laid eyes on her. That first day back in sixth grade
16  when Mrs. Peterson called the role and had us take our
17  seats in alphabetical order. I just knew it was a sign. And
18  she was so nice to me from day one. I remember thinking,
19  "A girl this beautiful can't be this nice." But she was. It was
20  like she didn't have a clue how great she looked or how
21  stupid I felt around her at first. I remember how she shared
22  her chocolate chip cookies with me on her birthday one year.
23  And she shared some funny jokes once in a while too. She
24  has this really amazing sense of humor. And she doesn't get
25  grossed out by the stuff that makes most girls sick. (Sighs.)
26  And I have always been certain that the Shephard-Shetfield
27  thing was a sign and that one day I'd get the nerve to ask
28  Miley out and the sparks would fly, you know? It would be
29  ... Kismet.

1      But last Friday, last Friday was probably the worst day
2  of my life. A new kid walked into home room about eight
3  fifteen. We had just said the pledge. He walked up to Mrs.
4  Peterson and she asked for his name. I heard him say
5  something that sounded like Shepman and I sort of got all
6  woozy, my ears started ringing, and I couldn't seem to
7  breathe. Before I knew what was happening I had passed
8  out right there in class. When I came to someone was wiping
9  my head with a cool towel. I heard myself saying, "Miley?"
10  But when I opened my eyes it was Mrs. Peterson. She was
11  hovering over me and wiping the water from my face.
12  Someone had thrown what seemed like a bucket of water on
13  my head. I lifted myself up to see if what I'd heard, what I'd
14  seen, had been just a terrible dream, but no. I dragged
15  myself up to go take my new seat behind Peter Shepman.
16  Miley was gone. She was one whole seat away and in home
17  room that's practically, well, a distant planet. Yup, I know
18  everything there is to know about Miley Shephard, but with
19  each passing day, she'll grow to be only a faint memory. It's
20  true. I know.

# 33. Weird

1    I fall for girls for really weird reasons. Yeah, weird. And I
2    always have. I mean, all the way back when I was three.
3    Yeah, when I was three. There was this girl named Pauline
4    Micheletti. She was in the first grade with my brother
5    Steven, so she was, like, a much older woman, you know.
6    *(Chuckles.)*
7    No, but seriously, I had this gigantic crush on Pauline
8    Micheletti. And you know why? I liked the way she chewed
9    her gum. Yeah, her gum. I liked the way she chewed her gum
10   on one side of her mouth, kind of like this. *(Demonstrates.)*
11   That was, like, so cool to me, and I was like head over heals
12   gaga for her. Yeah, gaga.
13   So, anyway, it's never changed. I always have and still
14   do fall for girls for weird reasons. A more recent example?
15   OK, I'll give you a more recent example. I can give you an
16   example as recent as last week. Cheerleader tryouts. Yeah,
17   cheerleader tryouts. I went to watch because my sister
18   Serafina was trying out. Yeah, Serafina. She didn't make it,
19   of course. She's too heavy for cheerleading. My mother
20   didn't have the heart to tell her and I didn't either, so I went
21   to support her. I give her credit for trying. Yeah, for trying.
22   So, anyway, I'm sitting there waiting for Serafina to get
23   called up and they call up this girl Lindsey Finger. Yeah,
24   Finger. So, I'm watching this girl and I'm thinking nothing
25   of it. But then they ask her to cheer with three other girls.
26   You know, to see how she works in a group. Yeah, a group.
27   So, I'm like, OK, this should be sort of interesting, but I'm
28   really just waiting to see Serafina and praying that she's not

1  going to make too much of a fool of herself. 'Cause it would
2  break my heart. Yeah, my heart.
3  So, anyway, this girl, Lindsey Finger, goes over and does
4  a cheer with these three other girls and she's really good,
5  but every time she does a jump or a turn or a flip-dee-do or
6  whatever you call it, she's always just about a beat late. So,
7  it was really funny, you know? And kind of cute. Yeah, cute.
8  So, that was it. What do you mean what was it? That was
9  it! I fell in love with Lindsey Finger because she's always a
10 beat behind the rest of the girls. Weird, right? Yeah, weird.

# 34. Keep Out

1    Look, I have a piece of advice for you. If you know what's
2    good for you, you'll stay out of my business. That's right.
3    Stay out of my business or there'll be some pretty serious
4    consequences. I'm not gonna tell you what those are. Those
5    are for me to know and you to find out, wise guy.
6        But I will tell you something. I don't trust you. Nah, I
7    don't trust you. And this whole stepbrother thing, this is
8    like, for the birds. You don't just become somebody's
9    brother overnight. Nah. A brother is somebody you can
10   trust. Somebody who proves themselves to you by always
11   stickin' by you and you always stick by them. To me, a
12   brother is like your friend in the face of an enemy. And kid,
13   you got a long ways to go before I can call you brother. And
14   in the meantime, like I said, stay out of my business. Stay
15   out of my bedroom, stay away from my car. If I go in that
16   garage and find even so much as a fingerprint on that car,
17   I'll know who it belongs to. Yeah, you. That's right. And that
18   will make me — how should I put this? — extremely
19   unhappy. And that's not good. You don't want that, little
20   man. You don't mind if I call you little man, do you? I mean,
21   you're kind of short for your age, aren't you? How old are you
22   anyway? This many? How many is this many? Tree? Oh, you
23   mean three? Are you sure? You look a lot older than that.
24   You wouldn't lie to me, would you? Well, listen little man,
25   like I said, you stay out of my business, I'll stay out of yours,
26   and we'll be just fine.

# 35. We've Come a Long Way

1    *(ROBERT enters the room, slams the door, and screams.) I*
2    *hate you! (He goes over to the desk and pushes the book off.)*
3    **And I hate school.** *(Sits on the bed, puts his head in his hands,*
4    *then looks up as if he's suddenly realizing something.)* **I'm a**
5    **prisoner. I'm a prisoner in my own home. And I'm a prisoner**
6    **at school. That yellow school bus should have a sign painted**
7    **on it in big black letters, "Prisoner Transport. Stay back fifty**
8    **feet."** *(Looks at the door and yells toward it.) I'm a prisoner in*
9    *here! Are you listening, Mother?*
10   *(Gets up and paces around the room.)* **How did it get like**
11 **this?** *(Looks at the audience.)* **How did it come to this? All we**
12 **do anymore is yell at each other.** *(Goes over to the door, opens*
13 *it, and yells out.) All you ever do is yell at me! (Slams the door*
14 *again. To himself and then to the audience)* **She doesn't care.**
15 **She doesn't care about me anymore. What happened? It**
16 **used to be so different. Soooo different. My mother and I**
17 **were like** *(Crosses fingers)* **this. We used to have the best of**
18 **times. But over the years, stuff has happened, I guess.**
19 *(Shrugs.)* **I've gotten older and she can't handle it. She still**
20 **wants to control every moment of my existence. That was**
21 **fine when I was a kid, but I'm a man now. I mean, OK, I'm**
22 **a teenager, but come on, can't she at least treat me like a**
23 **man? The way she talks to me ... the way I talk to her.**
24 **Things have really gotten out of hand. It's like, from the way**
25 **we were to the way things are, we've come a long way, man.**
26 **The only problem is we went the wrong direction**

# 36. Spring Break

1     Every year they descend upon us. The Spring Breakers.
2 Living in Panama City has its pros and its cons, but for me,
3 Spring Breakers are definitely one of the perks. I've been
4 enjoying their presence in my hometown every year since I
5 can remember. Well, from the first time I spent my summer
6 with my Uncle Harold selling snow cones on the beach,
7 when I was five-years-old to be exact. That was my initiation
8 to spring break. I remember all the girls used to say, "Oh,
9 he's so cute!"
10     Now my best friend Alfredo and I hit the beach every
11 spring break. It's amazing how every year the excitement is
12 there. The beautiful girls, the crazy college guys, the
13 partying, and just these masses of people. I don't really
14 take part in any of the crazy stuff that goes on. Neither does
15 Alfredo. We're sort of spectators, you might say. And there
16 is a lot to spectate, if you know what I mean. Nah, we don't
17 really get in on any of the stuff. We just enjoy the view.
18 Maybe, one day, when we're in college, we'll come back and
19 be party animals and all that.
20     If we go to college, that is. Alfredo isn't really on the
21 college track and even though I am, I'm not exactly
22 scholarship material and my folks can't afford to pay, so ...
23 maybe it will be community college and I'll stay right here in
24 town. At least I won't have to spend anything on spring
25 break. I'll just hit the beach in my own backyard, so to
26 speak. I wonder if it will ever get old? I guess it probably
27 won't until I get old, right? It's weird to think of getting old.
28 Sometimes I sit and look at all the tan bodies on the beach.

1 Bikinis, thongs, you name it, and I do this weird fast forward
2 in my mind. I'll think of stuff like, OK, fast forward fifty
3 years. Who will they all be? What will they all look like? It's
4 weird. I don't know where I come up with stuff like that. It's
5 kind of freaky, right? But it's true. In fifty years, we'll all be
6 old. Crazy to think of it now though, right? *(Laughs.)* I
7 wonder if I'll still be heading over to the beach on spring
8 break when I'm like a hundred and five. Maybe. Who knows.
9 Aw, who am I kidding? I do know. If I'm alive, I'll be there.
10 With my sunglasses on. I just hope I have enough sense not
11 to wear a thong.

# 37. Are You Awake?

1    *(Sits and looks over at "Johnathan's" cot.)* **Psssst. Psssst.**
2    **Hey, Johnathan. Hey, Johnathan. Are you awake?**
3    **Johnathan?** *(Gently nudges "Johnathan's" cot with his foot.)*
4    **Johnathan, are you awake?** *("Johnathan" answers groggily*
5    *that he is awake.)* **Oh, me too. I can't sleep.** *(Sighs.)* **It's this**
6    **place. It's giving me the creeps. Johnathan? Did you go**
7    **back to sleep? Johnathan?** *(Coughs loudly.)* **Oh, hey, you're**
8    **awake. No, I didn't wake you up. No. I just coughed. Did I?**
9    **Oh, sorry. I'll try to cough more quietly next time.**
10    **Hey, but since you're awake, what do you think of this**
11    **place? Yeah, what do you think? I think it's really weird. It's**
12    **like something out of a horror movie. That guy that brought**
13    **in the cot is really weird, don't you think? You didn't notice?**
14    **How could you not notice? Yeah, I was tired, too, but I still**
15    **noticed. I can't go back to sleep. If I could go back to sleep,**
16    **I'd already be sleeping and we wouldn't be having this**
17    **conversation. Yeah, OK, fine, go back to sleep. I don't know**
18    **how you can, but go right ahead. Don't let me stop you.**
19    *(Lays down and turns on his side, then suddenly sits up.)* **What**
20    **was that? Johnathan.** *(Kicks the cot.)* **Johnathan, wake up.**
21    **Did you hear that? That noise? It was like this.** *(Makes a*
22    *really weird sound.)* **Didn't you hear it? Yeah, well, I don't**
23    **know how you could sleep through a noise like that. I can't**
24    **go back to sleep. Yeah, yeah, yeah, I won't bother you again.**
25    **Hey, I just thought you might have heard it too. Yeah, yeah,**
26    **yeah, never mind. Go back to sleep.**
27    *(Looks at "Johnathan.")* **So, what are you waiting for?**
28    **What do you mean you don't think you can now? Of course**

1  you can. Just lie down and close your eyes and you'll be
2  snoring in two seconds. Uh-huh, snoring. Yes, you do. Yes,
3  you do. Johnathan, you snore. You do too. What does it
4  sound like? *(Thinks for a second.)* OK. It sounds like this.
5  *(Imitates the snore.)* Oh, yes it does. Hey, I ought to know. I'm
6  the one that can hear it. You're too busy sleeping. And
7  snoring. Oh yes, you do. Me? No, I don't. I know for one
8  hundred percent sure that I don't. Because I filmed myself.
9  Yeah, I did. I set up the camera on a tripod last month to
10 see if I snored. No, I did not. Look, I can show you the
11 movie. Go ahead, get out your laptop. It's on the web. Yes.
12 You can find my video on the web. What's it called? It's
13 called "Me, Not Snoring." Hey, forget about it. I'm going
14 back to sleep. Maybe now that you can't sleep I'll get some
15 rest. Yeah. Now that you're awake, your snoring won't wake
16 me up. Yeah, well, we can set up the camera tomorrow night
17 and you'll see. Yeah, yeah, whatever. I'm tired. Good night.
18 *(Lies down. Looks over one last time.)* And try not to wake me
19 up.

# 38. The Middle Child

1     Being the middle child isn't so bad. I'm the middle of five
2 kids in our family. I have an older brother and sister and a
3 younger brother and sister. And I'm in the middle. Not so
4 bad, right? I think for the most part we all get treated
5 equally, and you'd pretty much never know that I'm in the
6 middle. Oh yeah, there's been a few times when it might
7 have looked like I was being treated differently. You know,
8 all those middle child syndrome things, like not getting
9 enough attention and all that.
10     Well, I'll give you one example that might have been
11 labeled by some psychobabble freak as a middle child thing.
12 Last summer, my dad was working really hard. You know, a
13 lot of overtime, hardly ever getting a day off. That kind of
14 thing. So, finally, he begged his boss and he got the
15 weekend off so that we could go on this trip to go rafting on
16 the Lehigh River. We were all really excited about the rafting
17 and Mom was happy because we were gonna be able to stop
18 at Grandma's house on the way. So we did. We stopped at
19 Grandma's house and had some lunch. Then, I was real
20 tired, so I went in her extra bedroom and laid down and fell
21 asleep. Well, when I woke up it was dark outside. The phone
22 was ringing and it was Mom. They were in the motel and
23 they realized that they'd forgotten me. There wasn't time to
24 come back and get me and all that, so I went ahead and
25 spent the weekend with Grandma. They remembered to
26 stop by and pick me up on the way back, though. It sounded
27 like the rafting was a lot of fun. If we ever get to go again I
28 won't lay down, even if I'm really tired. In fact, I don't think

1    I'll even go in Grandma's house if we stop by. I'll just wait
2    in the car. That whole thing was not a middle child thing,
3    though. That could have happened to any of us kids. Really.
4    I think. Don't you?

# 39. Welcome to Wanda and Wally's World

1      Welcome to Wanda and Wally's World, may I take your
2    order? *(Writing it down)* OK, that's one Wanda Burger well
3    done with a large order of cheese fries. Do you want all the
4    stuff that comes on the burger, sir? Well, it comes with
5    lettuce, tomato, mushrooms, cheddar cheese, and a squirt
6    of mustard. OK, if you want onions, then that's a Wally
7    Burger. Yep, the Wanda burger doesn't come with any
8    onions, sir. No, sir. You can't. No, you can't add onions to a
9    Wanda burger, sir, because Wanda hates onions. Wanda
10   wouldn't be caught dead with onions on her burger, sir. OK.
11   Let me make sure I've got this right. *(Crosses off, erases, etc.,*
12   *and rewrites.)* You want a Wally Burger well done with a large
13   order of cheese fries. Is that correct? OK great. Do you want
14   all the stuff that comes on the burger, sir? Well, the Wally
15   burger comes with lettuce, tomato, onions, mushrooms,
16   ketchup, mustard, and Swiss cheese. No cheese? Oh, you
17   want the cheddar cheese? *(Aggravated)* On your Wally
18   burger? Sir, that's not an option on the Wally Burger. Well,
19   you can say "no cheese" on the Wally Burger, but you can't
20   put cheddar cheese on the Wally Burger. That's right, sir.
21   Wally can't stand cheddar cheese. If I tell the cook to put
22   cheddar on the Wally Burger he'll go ballistic. I'll tell you
23   what, how 'bout if I just bring you a Wanda Burger and I'll
24   slip you a side of onions when nobody's looking. Excuse me,
25   sir, but I'm not being difficult. Quite the contrary. I'm
26   offering to bring you onions when it could cost me my job.
27   OK, sir. *(Shaking his head and scratching out the order)* I'll just
28   bring you a grilled cheese. *(Walks away saying under his*
29   *breath)* Some people are so hard to please.

# 40. The Scoop

1       What's wrong with you, man? You think this job is
2  boring? Scooping ice cream is not so bad. Cheer up. You
3  have to make it fun. I have a few ways of making the time
4  go by. Well, one thing I do is I pretend I'm from a different
5  country sometimes. You know, put on an accent. Like I'm
6  from England or something. Watch, here comes a customer.
7  *(In English accent)* Cheerio, how are you on this lovely day,
8  madam? Jolly good. What flavor would you like?
9  Strawberry? Indeed? That is my favorite flavor. Will that be
10  two scoops or one? One scoop. Alrighty then. *(Scoops out the*
11  *ice cream.)* That will be three U.S. dollars. Oh, yes, I'm from
12  England, madam. That's correct. Very keen ear you have
13  young lady. *(Takes her money and puts it in the cash register. To*
14  *his friend without the accent)* You see, that was fun. Can you
15  do an accent or anything? You can? French? OK, let's hear
16  it. *(Listens and makes a face.)* Dude. I don't know what that
17  was, but it wasn't French.

18       Hmmmm. Maybe we need to find another way to make
19  it fun for you. Let's see. OK, all of the employees get to
20  come up with an ice cream special once a month, right?
21  They didn't tell you that? Oh, wow, OK, that's one of the
22  coolest things about this job. See, once a month, you get
23  to come up with some kind of ice cream concoction and the
24  manager will put it on the special board for, like, two dollars
25  and ninety-nine cents for one day. So, like, last month, I did
26  this thing I called Super Weird Strawberry Sundae. Yeah,
27  Super Weird. It was a big hit, too. The manager even said he
28  might repeat it this month. Oh man, it was so good, but it

1   was really weird. It was one scoop of strawberry ice cream
2   and two scoops of chocolate mint topped with caramel and
3   marshmallow cream. It was really popular. So, what would
4   your special be? Huh? Vanilla? You only like vanilla? Dude, I
5   strongly suggest you get a different job.

# 41. Shortcut

1     Aubrey, I need to tell you something. Promise you won't
2 tell Mom and Dad. *(Sighs.)* OK. You know that shortcut I
3 sometimes take home from school? Yeah, the one behind
4 the warehouses. Well, yesterday ... yesterday I took that
5 shortcut and I saw something that I wish I hadn't seen. You
6 swear you won't tell? OK. Well, I saw Tim and his brother
7 Eric, and it looked like they were stealing something. Yes,
8 stealing. It looked like they were stealing something from
9 that warehouse with all the car parts. Well, I was walking
10 and as soon as I saw them I kind of stopped dead in my
11 tracks and hid behind a bush. I can't stand Eric and he
12 hates me, so I really just didn't want to run into them, and
13 I was gonna turn around and just go the long way, but I was
14 kind of curious, so I watched.
15     *(Sighs.)* Man, I wish I had just turned right around.
16 'Cause now I saw them stealing stuff. They were hurrying
17 and looking around and looking all guilty and everything.
18 Then they heard someone coming and they took off in Eric's
19 car. You know, that old beat up Chevy that he drives. I don't
20 know what to do. I mean I feel like this makes me sort of an
21 accomplice. If I don't tell, that is. And, if I do tell, Tim and
22 Eric could get in some really serious trouble. Like go to jail.
23 Tim is my friend. Eric, well, obviously, I couldn't care less
24 what happens to him, but Tim? How can I turn him in? I'd
25 feel like such a traitor. And we're not talking just a little
26 thing like skipping class. This is major. And I can guarantee
27 you it wasn't his idea. His brother is the biggest jerk on the
28 planet. He probably made him do it. Oh geez, Aubrey, what

1  am I gonna do? What would you do? I sure wish that I'd
2  never taken that shortcut.

# 42. The Interview

1     Did you see it? The interview! They interviewed me on
2   the news last night! Channel four. You didn't see it? Oh,
3   wow, it was awesome! They interviewed me and Sam Miller.
4   Because we were volunteering for the walkathon. The
5   walkathon! You didn't hear about the walkathon? The whole
6   school was there practically. Yeah, *that* walkathon! The one
7   for Erica Cartwright. Wow, it was so cool. We were standing
8   there making peanut butter and jelly sandwiches for the
9   walkers. We had to make three hundred and forty-five
10  peanut butter and jelly sandwiches, so we had this whole
11  assembly line system down and we had music playing and
12  we were sort of bopping to the music and they caught the
13  whole thing on film and then they asked us a bunch of
14  questions and stuff.

15  Maybe they'll put it on the Internet. It was so cool. It was
16  that reporter, Mandy Stevenson. Yeah, the hot one. She is
17  even more hot in person. I think she has a crush on me.
18  Yeah, she smiled at me a whole lot. She hardly asked Sam
19  anything, but she asked me about a hundred questions. Uh-
20  huh. Like where do I go to school, why was I doing this, what
21  did I think of the turnout. Oh, and the best question was,
22  and she said it in this sexy voice, "Do you think you'll ever
23  want to see a peanut butter and jelly sandwich again?"
24  Yeah, she said it just like that. "Do you think you'll ever
25  want to see a peanut butter and jelly sandwich again?" I
26  said, "Not really." What else was I supposed to say?
27  Something funny? How can you answer that question in a
28  way that's funny? What would you have said? And that's

1    supposed to be funny? Do you see me laughing? That is so
2    not funny. Yeah, whatever. So, anyway, you're just changing
3    the subject because you're jealous. Because I got to talk to
4    Mandy Stevenson in person and she shook my hand. Well,
5    she didn't really shake it. She sort of squeezed it. Uh-huh. I
6    don't think I'll ever wash this hand again.

# 43. Superlatives

1    Who did you vote for? For superlatives. You know, "Most
2    Likely to Succeed" and "Most Talented." Yeah, that. Who
3    did you pick? You didn't do it yet? You better not wait too
4    long. I think the cut off day is March third.
5    Me? Well, I voted for Tara McNeal for "Best Dressed Girl"
6    and Jim Stevens for "Best Dressed Guy." Yeah, that was a
7    no-brainer. For "Most Likely to Succeed"? Well, that was a
8    hard one. I mean, I almost voted for Karen Brewer for "Most
9    Likely to Succeed" because she's such a good actress, but
10    then I decided to go with "Most Talented" for her. I could
11    have voted for her for both, but I got to thinking about it and
12    I really don't think she's the most likely to succeed. Well,
13    the thing is, she's very talented, but she's kind of egotistical
14    too. Well, that can be a good thing for an actress, but I think
15    it can also be a negative. For instance, she has a lot of
16    confidence for auditioning, which is good, but ... I'm not
17    sure that she really thinks she has any room for
18    improvement. She's just not open to getting any better,
19    right? She thinks she's it. And maybe she is the "It Girl" of
20    Seymour High, but when she gets out in the real world, is
21    she going to be able to sharpen her skills and compete? I
22    don't think so. But like I said, I voted for her for "Most
23    Talented" and I really think she is. Karen has all the raw
24    talent, the natural ability. But her attitude is what's gonna
25    make her shoot herself in the foot. Yep, that's my prediction.
26    But now Laura Saunders is a different story. She's not
27    as talented as Karen, but she works really, really hard. And
28    she is open to suggestions. She is gonna go out in the real

1   world and kick some butt. Yep, that's my prediction. Uh-
2   huh. I voted for Laura for "Most Likely to Succeed." You
3   think I'm wrong? Maybe, but if we bet on it, man, you know
4   what you are? "Most Likely to Lose."

# 44. If Money Grew on Trees

1    I love my mom, but sometimes she's a bit of a nag.
2  She's always got to give me advice — put in her two cents,
3  or pass down some words of wisdom. And some of her
4  sayings get kind of old after a while. Like whenever I want
5  to buy something she always says, "You know, money
6  doesn't grow on trees." If I had a nickel for every time she
7  said that, I'd be a guzillionaire.

8    *(Sighs.)* But boy, I sure do wish money did grow on trees.
9  Last night, it was kind of funny. All my mom's nagging
10  finally got to me. I had a dream that I was walking through
11  the backyard and there was money hanging off of all the tree
12  limbs. I was like, "Mom, come out here. There's something
13  that I want to show you." She came running out with my dad
14  and my little sister Lori. It was really cool. We were all
15  excited and happy and laughing. And I looked at my mom
16  and I said, "Mom, this time you're gonna have to admit
17  you're wrong." She was so happy, she didn't even care that
18  she was wrong. We were all grabbing that money and telling
19  each other what we were gonna do with it. I grabbed a bunch
20  of hundreds off the orange tree and I said, "I'm going over
21  to the computer store, does anybody want anything while
22  I'm there?" My mom said, "Sure, bring me one of those
23  laptops, will you?" I said, "OK," but when I woke up later,
24  it made me wonder if my mom really would like a laptop. I'm
25  always telling her what I want and what I need, but she
26  never says a thing about wanting anything. I just had to go
27  find out if she was really wanting a laptop all along and just
28  keeping it to herself, so I went out into the kitchen and

1  asked her. "Mom," I said, "I'll bet you'd like to have your
2  own personal laptop to use instead of always having to wait
3  for your turn to get on the family PC." She just looked at me
4  and rolled her eyes. Then she said, "Son, when are you ever
5  gonna remember what I've been trying to tell you for years?"
6  You guessed it. "Money doesn't grow on trees."

# 45. Friends Forever?

1       Here's your punch, Katie. Whew! It's hot out here, but
2 I'm glad you wanted to come outside for a bit. It's been a
3 great party, hasn't it? It sure was a good idea to get our
4 folks together for this graduation party. After all, we've been
5 best friends for how long now? Yep, since second grade.
6 That's a long time. *(Looks up at the sky.)* **Wow, there's a lot**
7 of stars out here tonight. It's beautiful, isn't it? You look
8 beautiful tonight too, Katie. No, I'm serious, you do. I never
9 told you that before so it probably sounds kind of weird
10 coming from me, but it's true. I should have told you that a
11 long time ago. Stop what? Being silly? I'm not being silly.
12 *(Sighs.)* **You know you're beautiful, right? Well, you are. But**
13 that's not all. You've got a lot of other good qualities, too.
14 Things that are more important than looks. I was thinking
15 about that the other day. Yeah, I really was. I don't know
16 why. I guess with graduation around the corner and all that.
17 I guess I'm just getting kind of sentimental or nostalgic or
18 something. I made a list of your good qualities. Want to hear
19 it? Aw, come on, it's the "Top Ten Best Qualities of Katie
20 Strawbaker." I've got it right here in my pocket. Yes, I did.
21 I wrote them all down.

22       *(Takes the list out and shows it to her.)* **See. You don't have**
23 to read them. I'll read them to you. Aw, come on Katie, for
24 me? OK. Here it goes. *(Stares at the paper while reading.)*
25 Good quality number ten: Katie always finds a way to make
26 me laugh. Quality number nine: Katie is sweet to my hound
27 dog Henry even though he usually smells. Number eight:
28 Katie likes to make you chicken noodle soup when you're

1 sick. Number seven: Katie makes the best chocolate chip
2 cookies I have ever had. Number six: Katie never minds
3 riding in my pickup truck, even when the bed is full of
4 manure. Number five: Katie always takes my side when I've
5 had an argument with my parents. Number four: Katie is the
6 smartest girl I know. Number three: Katie doesn't have to
7 talk about anything. She can just sit and be quiet with you
8 for a real long time. Number two: Katie will give you her last
9 nickel if you need it. Number one: Katie will act like she
10 doesn't know you've been madly in love with her for years,
11 just so you'll never have to feel like a fool. *(Finally gets the*
12 *nerve to look up.)* Katie, you're crying. Don't worry, I know. I
13 know you just want to be friends. I just ... I just want you
14 to know that I think the world of you, but ... I don't think I
15 can do it too much longer. I ... I don't think we can be
16 friends forever. Do you?

# 46. Who Are You?

1     Most kids don't really know what they want to do when
2 they grow up. I mean, from the time you can barely walk
3 people ask you that question. When you're in first grade
4 everybody wants to be a fireman, right? But not me. I kind
5 of always knew what I wanted to be. A psychologist. See,
6 my aunt is a psychologist and she raised me — pretty much.
7 My mom had me when she was real young. So most of the
8 time, growing up, I stayed at my aunt's. She had an office
9 in the back of the house and I used to play right nearby and
10 sometimes the door would be slightly open. I learned real
11 young that the biggest thing my aunt did was just listen.
12 And I like that. That's what I do best.
13     I'm a real quiet guy. And most people, they think I'm
14 just shy or that I'm kind of dim-witted. Not a whole lot goin'
15 on upstairs and all that. Lights are on, but nobody's home.
16 I've heard them say all those kinds of things about me when
17 they thought I wasn't listening. But that's their mistake.
18 'Cause I'm always listening and I'm always watching.
19 Observing, that is. And I can listen to you and observe you
20 and I'll bet you a million dollars that I can figure you out. I
21 can tell you who you are. And you know something, you may
22 think you know who you are and how you got that way, but
23 just about ninety-nine percent of the time, people don't
24 really know. I mean, what do you suppose you'd say if I
25 asked you, "Who are you?" You'd give me your name of
26 course. Then you'd probably tell me where you live and what
27 you do. Like go to school, or are a cheerleader, or some
28 nonsense like that. But who you are is a whole lot more than

1   that. And that is exactly what I want to help people figure
2   out. Who they are. Even though sometimes they may not
3   want to hear it.
4       Well, people with problems for instance. They don't
5   always want to know who they are. Well, like Leroy James.
6   Yeah, that guy that's always going around "kicking people's
7   butts." I've seen him around town and I've heard things
8   around town and I know who he is and why he is that way.
9   See, ever since he was little, Leroy's dad's been kicking his
10  butt. So Leroy, he's angry with his father, but he can't tell
11  him that. When he was little, he couldn't do much about it
12  anyway. So he takes his anger out on kids at school and
13  kids in the neighborhood. 'Cause he can't stand up to his
14  dad. But see, he won't stop this behavior until he realizes
15  who he is and why he's doing what he does. Then, if he
16  wants to change, he's gonna have to confront his dad. Yeah,
17  that's what I think. He doesn't have to fight him, but he has
18  to stand face-to-face with him and tell him what he thinks
19  of him and that he's not gonna take it anymore. But that's
20  hard for a kid. That's hard because his dad won't want to
21  listen and Leroy probably doesn't have any place else to go.
22  Or at least he thinks he doesn't.
23      But that's one of the things I'd do if I were a
24  psychologist. I'd help kids like Leroy to find a place, a safe
25  place from their parents. So they wouldn't have to be angry
26  all the time and they wouldn't have to run away. My auntie,
27  she works mostly with adults, but sometimes she has to
28  find them a safe place too. Especially some women so they
29  can get away from their husbands. I think some of those
30  husbands are people like Leroy. They just never confronted
31  the man that was beating down on them and now they act
32  like they don't have a brain in their head. They go through
33  their life letting somebody who hurt them a long time ago
34  decide who they are. And they don't even know that they
35  need help.

1     So, see, that's why I want to be a psychologist, so I can
2    help people understand who they are and how they got to be
3    that way. Then, if they want to change, I can help them. But
4    they have to want to change, you know? It's just like that
5    old phrase I heard my aunt say so many times when her
6    patients just wouldn't accept who they were and what they
7    needed to do. She'd come out of that office muttering, "You
8    can lead a horse to water, but you can't make him drink."
9    She didn't think I heard her, but then you know me, right?
10  I don't miss a thing.

# 47. Wishing You Were Here

1     *(Sitting with a shampoo bottle in his hands. Takes a whiff. To*
2     *the audience)* She's gone. And all I have left is this shampoo
3     bottle. *(Sighs.)* What a summer. The summer I'll never
4     forget. You see, six weeks ago my cousin Kelley came to
5     stay with us for a while. She asked my parents if she could
6     bring a friend and I remember thinking how crowded the
7     house was going to be and how I was going to try to find a
8     way to be busy all summer so I wouldn't have to be
9     entertaining the two "guests."
10    The first thing I had to do, of course, was pick them up
11   at the airport. I was kind of annoyed because a whole bunch
12   of my friends were going to the beach that day and I had to
13   drive all the way down to Miami International Airport to pick
14   up two spoiled brats. I mean, I knew my cousin Kelley would
15   be bringing about five pieces of designer luggage packed
16   with about five thousand bikinis with matching earrings and
17   flip-flops. She's always gotten whatever she wanted and
18   expects everyone to jump to her every need. So I could just
19   see myself walking behind her and some spoiled brat friend
20   with about fifty pieces of luggage piled on me and under me
21   and the two of them making me their personal servant and
22   all that.
23    But the minute they stepped off the plane, all those
24   thoughts vanished. Walking just behind Kelley was the most
25   beautiful girl I had ever seen. And as soon as she looked at
26   me she smiled her beautiful warm Georgia smile and our
27   eyes sort of locked. Yeah, it was love at first sight. Kelley
28   didn't even notice because she was yammering on and on

1   about the flight and how the air in the plane was so bad for
2   her hair and her complexion and when did I think I could
3   take them to the beach and blah, blah, blah and on and on
4   forever. But her friend, Marissa ... Marissa Samantha
5   Smith. She and I never stopped looking at each other. Well,
6   except when I was driving of course. But even then, I kept
7   looking in the rearview mirror.
8       We went back to the house and they changed into their
9   swim stuff. I took them to the beach and that was it. After
10  that afternoon, Marissa and I were together. I know it made
11  Kelley really mad 'cause she had all these plans to hang out,
12  just the two girls. But that just wasn't meant to be. *(Smells*
13  *the shampoo again and sighs.)* Yesterday I had to take them
14  to the airport for the flight home. Marissa cried. Well, I
15  mean, she didn't bawl or anything like that, but I saw a tear
16  in her left eye. When I got back to the house I felt alone. I
17  didn't think there was a trace of Marissa left, but then I
18  found this. *(Looks at the bottle.)* This smells just like her.
19  *(Reads the bottle.)* Summer Breeze shampoo. *(Holds it to his*
20  *chest.)* Marissa, I miss you.

# 48. The Finish Line

1   I have a problem with endings. *(Sighs.)* No, I don't mean
2   like happy endings or sad endings in movies or stories. No.
3   I mean I don't like those either, but that's really not what
4   I'm talking about. What I'm talking about is a real problem.
5   You know, of the psychological nature, I guess. I just can't
6   stand ending anything. Well, I guess you might say finishing
7   anything.

8       OK, for example, last night I sat at the dining room table
9   doing my math homework. And let me tell you, I actually
10  love math. My teacher, Mrs. Firestoop, is hot. But that's not
11  why I love math. I love it because I'm good at it. So, anyway,
12  here I am sitting there at the dining room table doing my
13  math homework and munching on Mom's special vanilla
14  chocolate chip brownies. I was really rocking and rolling and
15  then, I looked down at the book and there they were. The
16  last three problems. Three more problems between me and
17  finishing my homework. You might think that's a good thing,
18  but for me ... that sight put me into a complete sweat. I
19  mean, what if I've gotten this close and then I didn't get to
20  finish. Like, what if I have a complete breakdown or choke
21  on a brownie, or barf all over all the other problems and the
22  whole thing is down the toilet?

23      These are the kinds of thoughts that go through my
24  mind. All rational fears, right? But only a crazy guy like me
25  would have them. The same thing happens to me on tests
26  in class. I start out like I'm breezing through it and all that
27  and then I start getting toward the end and I get the shakes.
28  If I have, like, only two questions to go before the end, I'll

1   suddenly get the urge to run to the bathroom. And it's either
2   finish the last two questions and explode all over the
3   classroom, or run to the can and get the last two questions
4   wrong, because I didn't answer them. I didn't finish. You
5   understand, don't you? The pressure this kind of situation
6   puts me in? I mean, right now, I'm getting a little nervous
7   because this monologue doesn't last too much longer, and
8   if I only have two or three lines to go, I just might spew. Oh,
9   my goodness, here it comes ...

# 49. One Summer Day

1    You did what? You let them go? Why? What were you
2    thinking? You mean it? You're not kidding? Oh, man. Why?
3    I just don't get it. We spent hours collecting those snakes!
4    Hours! Days! We spent hours making the cage. You didn't
5    let 'em all go, did you? Why? Can't you just have the
6    decency to tell me that? That's the least you can do. You
7    had a dream? A dream that all the snakes were coming after
8    you? So? Dude, it was a dream! Man, all that work. All those
9    really cool snakes. We'll never find those again. I don't
10   know.

11   *(Sighs.)* What do you want to do now? I came over here
12   to look at the snakes. So, what are we going to do now? All
13   that work. A week's worth of work. All undone in one day.
14   Couldn't you have at least asked me first? I was half owner,
15   man. Yeah, I know they were in your yard. But I caught at
16   least half of them. I let them stay in your yard. I could've
17   taken them home if I'd wanted to. I would have put them in
18   the pool, that's where. Aw, man, why are we even bothering
19   to talk about it? It doesn't matter what I think. It's all about
20   you. You think you're a guy's friend. You think you
21   understand a person and he understands you and then ... a
22   day comes like today. You wake up and you look out your
23   window. It looks like any other day, but this day, this one
24   particular summer day, is the day that you're going to find
25   out that the guy that you thought was your friend, your best
26   friend, stabs you in the back. Yeah, right in the back. And
27   it hurts, man. I can't lie. I mean, I'm a tough guy. You know
28   I am. But even a guy like me has feelings too. Even a guy

1 like me can feel some pain. Man, oh man. All that work, all
2 those plans. All those snakes. Gone in a minute. All
3 because of a dream. A dream! Man.
4     *(Sighs.)* So, you haven't answered my question yet. What
5 are we gonna do now? Grasshoppers? *(Thinks about it for a*
6 *second.)* Grasshoppers. Yeah. OK. Cool, let's go.

# 50. I Fly

1     What's it like to be happy? Do you know? Are *you*
2 happy?
3     I watch people. I study them. I want to know. I want to
4 *see* if I can somehow *feel* their happiness. I'll tell you what I
5 see. I see people laughing. I see people acting up. But I don't
6 see sincere. You know what I mean? I don't see sincere, *real*
7 happy people. One in a hundred, maybe. One in a thousand!
8 A lot of people acting. People ... they want you to think they
9 got it goin' on. But half the time ... it ain't for real. You're
10 gonna think I'm strange, but I think about it *all* the time.
11 When you can't have something, you think about it all the
12 time, right? So, I think about how it would feel to be happy.
13 I think about it twenty-four hours a day. Seven days a week.
14 Like your corner convenience store. Only, it ain't so
15 convenient, right?
16     I had a dream once that I was ... I was in a plane. I'm
17 sitting at the steering wheel and there are people, you know,
18 friends, and they're getting into the plane to ride with me.
19 I'm the pilot and I'm like, "You don't have to be afraid 'cause
20 I've done this before." And everybody gets in and we take
21 off. And I fly. I fly and I feel ... so happy.
22     When I woke up, for like five seconds, I still felt it. For
23 five seconds, some sort of happiness. *(Pause)* Sometimes I
24 look at pictures in magazines. Celebrities, models. I look at
25 them and I wonder, "What must it be like to feel so good
26 inside? To have so much to live for?" I wonder if they even
27 know how good it is. What they have. I wonder if they take
28 it for granted. I look at those pictures and I close my eyes

1   and I say to myself, "If you ever wake up one day and you
2   have a reason to smile like that, don't you ever forget what
3   it was like when you didn't. If you ever wake up and feel
4   happy, you better appreciate it. If you ever, ever feel it for
5   real, you better treat it like gold." Do I believe that day will
6   ever come? *(Shakes his head.)* If I told you any different, I'd
7   be lying. And that is one thing that I won't do. I won't lie
8   and I won't pretend. But sometimes ... sometimes I close
9   my eyes and remember that dream. I close my eyes and I
10  see myself climbing into that cockpit. I see myself taking
11  control ... and I fly.

# About the Author

Mary holds a B.A. in Acting/Directing from Florida Atlantic University where she studied with Edward Albee and Joshua Logan. She also studied opera and performed in *The Medium* by Carlo Menotti and *La Serva Padrona* by Giovanni Battista Pergolesi.

Mary taught drama for ten years and has directed and performed in countless plays.

Mary's published writings include *Sugared and Spiced: 100 Monologues for Girls* and *Echo Booming Monologues: 100 Monologues for Teens,* both published by Jelliroll, Inc. Mary is delighted to be published with Meriwether and looks forward to writing many more books in the future.

In addition to writing for the stage, Mary enjoys singing, reading, and watching independent and foreign films.

# Order Form

**Meriwether Publishing Ltd.**
PO Box 7710
Colorado Springs, CO 80933-7710
Phone: 800-937-5297  Fax: 719-594-9916
Website: www.meriwether.com

*Please send me the following books:*

_____  **50/50 Monologues for Student Actors**          $15.95
**#BK-B321**
by Mary Depner
*100 monologues for guys and girls*

_____  **102 Great Monologues  #BK-B315**                $16.95
by Rebecca Young
*A versatile collection of monologues and duologues for student actors*

_____  **Famous Fantasy Character Monologs**              $15.95
**#BK-B286**
by Rebecca Young
*Starring the Not-So-Wicked Witch and more*

_____  **100 Great Monologs  #BK-B276**                   $15.95
by Rebecca Young
*A collection of monologs, duologs and triologs for actors*

_____  **Winning Monologs for Young Actors**              $15.95
**#BK-B127**
by Peg Kehret
*Honest-to-life monologs for young actors*

_____  **Young Women's Monologs from**                    $15.95
**Contemporary Plays  #BK-B272**
edited by Gerald Lee Ratliff
*Professional auditions for aspiring actresses*

_____  **Improv Ideas  #BK-B283**                         $23.95
by Justine Jones and Mary Ann Kelley
*A book of games and lists*

**These and other fine Meriwether Publishing books are available at
your local bookstore or direct from the publisher. Prices subject to
change without notice. Check our website or call for current prices.**

Name: _____ email:_____

Organization name: _____

Address: _____

City: _____ State: _____

Zip: _____ Phone: _____

❑  **Check enclosed**

❑  **Visa / MasterCard / Discover / Am. Express #** _____

*Signature:* _____  Expiration date: _____ / _____
(required for credit card orders)

**Colorado residents:** Please add 3% sales tax.
**Shipping:** Include $3.95 for the first book and 75¢ for each additional book ordered.

❑  *Please send me a copy of your complete catalog of books and plays.*